Leaping

revelations *and* epiphanies

BRIAN DOYLE

LOYOLAPRESS.

CHICAGO

LOYOLAPRESS.

3441 N. ASHLAND AVENUE
CHICAGO, ILLINOIS 60657
(800) 621-1008
WWW.LOYOLABOOKS.ORG

The Bible excerpts in "Why Write?" and "Grace Notes" are taken from the King James Bible (Cambridge University Press).

The Bible excerpts in "Room Eight," "Washed Clean," "Christ's Elbows," and "Altar Boy" are taken from the Revised Standard Version of the Bible, copyright © 1946, 1952, and 1971 by the Division of Christian Education of the National Council of the Churches of Christ in the USA.

The Bible excerpt in "Leap" is taken from the *New American Bible with Revised New Testament and Revised Psalms,* copyright © 1991, 1986, 1970 by the Confraternity of Christian Doctrine, Washington, D.C. Used with permission. All rights reserved. No part of the *New American Bible* may be reproduced by any means without permission in writing from the copyright owner.

The excerpt on pages 36–37 is taken from Louise Erdrich, *The Blue Jay's Dance: A Birth Year* (New York: HarperCollins, 1995), 70–72. Copyright © 1995 by Louise Erdrich.

The letter on pages 58–60 is reprinted by permission of Jim Wood.

The excerpt on page 105 is taken from Walt Whitman's "The Dalliance of the Eagles," *Leaves of Grass* (Philadelphia: David McKay, 1900).

Cover and interior design by Megan Duffy Rostan

Cover photo: © Clarissa Leahy/Getty Images

Author photo: Jerome Hart Photography

Library of Congress Cataloging-in-Publication Data
Doyle, Brian, 1956–
  Leaping : Revelations & Epiphanies / Brian Doyle.
    p. cm.
  ISBN 0-8294-1813-X
  1. Religious life. I. Title.
  BL624.D69 2003
  242—dc21

                     2003006634

Printed in the United States of America
03 04 05 06 07 08 09 10 Bang 10 9 8 7 6 5 4 3 2 1

for Mary

CONTENTS

A Note

These pieces first emerged publicly (blinking unsteadily) in a pile of really interesting magazines and newspapers, and it would be a selfish burro of a man who would not pause here and bow gently to the editors of the *American Scholar*, the *Atlantic Monthly*, the *Georgia Review*, *Harper's*, *Commonweal*, *Orion*, *U.S. Catholic*, *Portland Magazine*, *Notre Dame Magazine*, the *Catholic Sentinel*, *Boston College Magazine*, *Creative Nonfiction*, *Oregon Humanities*, *America*, *Ar Mhuin na Muice*, and the *Age* (in Melbourne, Australia), where many of these stories appeared, in sometimes hilariously different forms.

My thanks especially to Anne Fadiman, Terry Hummer, Elizabeth Giddens, Peggy Steinfels, Chip Blake, Cathy O'Connell-Cahill, Tom McGrath, Kerry Temple, Bob Pfohman, my inky brother Ben Birnbaum, Kathleen Holt, my musical brother Mick Mulcrone, and my antipodean brother James Button for their kindness and counsel and utter lack of fussy copyediting.

Also I wouldn't have written ten good sentences in ten years without my extraordinary lithe exuberant subtle wife, and God alone knows what self-indulgent asinine muck I would have written without the wild stimulus of our children, so to my wife and daughter and twin sons I say this: thank you. I love you more than I can understand.

—Brian Doyle

I Believe

C redo, Latin for "I believe," which I do, very strongly, in a
number of things.

I believe that there is a mysterious and graceful and miraculous
Coherence stitched through this world.

I believe that this life is an extraordinary gift, a blink of bright
light between vast darknesses.

I believe that the fingerprints of the Maker are everywhere:
children, hawks, water.

I believe that even sadness and tragedy and evil are part of that
Mind we cannot comprehend but only thank, a Mind especially to
be thanked, oddly, when it is most inscrutable.

I believe that children are hilarious and brilliant mammals.

I believe that everything is a prayer.

I believe that my wife is the strongest and most graceful female
being I have ever met, with the possible exception of my mother.

I believe that a family is a peculiar and powerful corporation,
lurching toward light, webbed by love, a whole ridiculously bigger
than its parts.

I believe, additionally, that friends are family.

I believe, deeply and relievedly, in giggling.

I believe that the best of all possible breakfasts is a pear with a
cup of ferocious coffee, taken near the ocean, rather later in the

morning than earlier, preferably in the company of a small sleepy child still in her or his rumpled and warm pajamas, his or her skin as warm and tawny as a cougar pelt.

I believe that love is our greatest and hardest work.

Why Write?

S ome months ago I saw an amateur play in a small theater. The play was forgettable except for one extraordinary moment: near the end of the second act a very large young man stepped forward into the glare of the footlights and began to sing. He was wearing a glittering ballroom gown, his face was heavily painted, and he was sweating so profusely that his wig had wigged out. The song was execrable and his voice a groaning tractor.

But I sat there riveted, and so did the rest of the small audience, and when that enormous young man finished his voyage through that thin song, we roared our delight. Somehow he had taken dreck and made of it art; he had made us believe, against all evidence and sense, that he was indeed a lovelorn girl a century ago. Whatever it is exactly that enables a superb actor to command rapt attention, to bewizard a roomful of people into believing the unbelievable, this kid had it in spades.

To execute his peculiar role he must have spent many hours learning his lines, practicing his song, memorizing the blocking and staging of the play, rehearsing with the ensemble. On that night he had caked his face with oily muck, donned an unfortunate wig, struggled into a dress the size of a tent, and presented himself in glaringly bright light before a scant audience who had every right to howl with laughter. And then, with stunning aplomb, he had drawn the men and women in the theater into his imagination.

The self-possession of this boy, not yet twenty!

One moment above all others stays with me from that night: in the instant between the end of his song and the rising roar in the little theater he stepped back a bit from the light and grinned—with relief, certainly, but also with something subtler. I think it was a deep humming joy that he had done what he had dreamed of doing. He had, for a few moments in a dark theater on a rainy night, created something with his body and voice and presence and conviction that would seem, given this particular act and actor, uncreatable.

He had made something wonderful of nothing but dreaming and labor and passion, something that probably not even he knew he could make with such eerie skill—and that is where I wish to begin talking about creativity, for dreaming and labor and passion are its ingredients, and wonder is both its engine and its product.

I am a small writer—a slight man much given to writing brief essays in small rooms. I look over the essays I have published over the course of twenty years of diligent scribbling and am astonished at their riotous incoherence. Here are some recent subjects: baptism, chickens, kneeling, Plutarch, foxes, dirt, crucifixes, car crushing, anchovies, tigers, summer, the legendary lost memoir of the late jazz saxophonist Paul Desmond, angels, knives, the Irish hero Cú Chulainn, grace, philately, hell, and silence. If there is a theme in all this it completely eludes the author, who feels that he has wandered into a pathless forest and is thrashing his way home armed with only a pen.

Which is sort of the point. Thrashing toward light with a sharp pen is what writers do. From the vast muddle and slew of facts and people around them they pick out threads of stories and then try to weave the threads together, each in his or her own way—articles, essays, novels, short stories, interviews, letters, poems, songs, profiles, monologues, plays, editorials, books, travelogues, diaries, journals, speeches, rants, etc.

Why?

Not for money—the great majority of people who write don't make money, and to sail into the craft to get rich is a fool's voyage.

Not for fame—the great majority of those who write are either little known or unknown hoping to be little known.

Why then? Why do I write?

Because I see little stories everywhere and I like to catch them and show them to other people much as a child catches a moth and exhibits it with glee to friends and passersby.

Because, as the fine essayist E. M. Forster (who also committed novels, the poor man) said, "How can I know what I think until I see what I say?" which is a very wise thing to say.

Because there have been times in my life when the only way I could handle rage and horror and fear was to write it down and thus fend it off, fight it, force it to retreat, understand it, hurt it.

Because like all human beings I have an innate drive to leave something shapely and permanent behind me, some marker of passage through the woods. Some of us build houses, companies, reputations, tribes of children; some of us make small essays in small rooms. I'd like to leave several books behind me so that someday my children will open and read them and think maybe the old man actually had a fastball for a while there.

Because writing is a form of contemplation and a form of prayer.

Because writing occasionally leads to rapture.

Because writing is a way to connect electrically and directly with other people, which we crave, while generally preserving privacy, which we also crave. ("Do I contradict myself? Very well, then, I contradict myself," wrote Walt Whitman.)

Because writing is a form of performance that does not demand physical grace or youth, and writers, despite their craving for privacy, like to be the center of attention, usually intermittently, rather than continually like film stars and Bill Clinton.

Because writers are, deep in their souls, didacts who itch to deliver the Unvarnished Truth and cannot help but unburden themselves of that which burns in their hearts. Writers are preachers.

*

The pithiest explanation for writing I ever heard was from the late growling crusty wonderful novelist George Higgins of Boston, who had, as he said, done actual work (as a district attorney prosecuting the Mafia in New England) before becoming a novelist, and so had no patience for enervated talk of, as he snarled, "art, aesthetics, and other crap about literature with a capital *L*." Writing, he said, was a benign neurosis—something you were quietly driven to do. You either did it or you didn't, and all talk about it was beside the point.

After I graduated from Notre Dame, a hundred years ago, I had a conversation with my father that I remember vividly.

"Now that you are fully educated," said my quiet father one summer day, "what are you going to do?"

"I'm going to be a writer," I said confidently.

"Great," said my father, who is a fine writer. "Want some advice? Get a job, learn to type, read like a fiend, and learn to be quiet."

"Thanks," I said, puzzled, flip, silently dismissive.

Pause.

"Did you write today?" he asked suddenly.

"Well, no—I played basketball, and . . ."

"Then you're not going to be a writer."

I thought he was cruel and dismissive himself, that day, and I was hurt; clearly he didn't see my talent, my potential, my drive. But he was right, and wise, and even gentle. He was telling me the truth in his quiet direct honest way, which is the way he loves. He was telling me that a fine writer writes all the time, thinks about writing, thinks like a writer, dreams stories, sees stories, smells them, is spinning them in his head all the time, has snatches of stories in his pockets, tells stories, collects stories, is alert to stories, is always itching to get to a typewriter and start to shape those stories, because maybe this story will sing, and maybe if I work hard enough it'll pour out straight and true and strong, and it'll *matter*, it'll *change* things, it'll hit people in the heart, it'll make them cry, change the way someone acts, stop a man from cracking his son across the face, give a moment of quivering tranquility to a woman in despair, make a girl laugh.

You never know.

*

All men and women and children are creative, especially mothers and teachers. A poet friend of mine goes further and says that not only are all people creative but most people spend their creative energy trying not to be creative—filling their time almost desperately with work or distraction, anything to keep them from facing the fact that there is a part of them that wishes to shape and make, to dream and putter.

I'm not sure. I agree that all people are creative, but it seems to me that (a) many people are creative in ways that don't fit the orthodox artistic examples of the urge—e.g., cooks, carpenters, gardeners, engineers, politicians, professors, detectives; and (b) most people in the world are creative in trying to find food, protect themselves from danger, seek shelter, evade war, find clean water, get through the day without too much damage.

The vast majority of the world's creativity is burned up in try-ing to survive. In the same way that abortion kills not only what is but also what might have been, so do war and corporate greed and political cupidity and ethnic solipsism kill what might have been, an incalculable loss.

To remove this from the general: Mao starved thirty million people between 1958 and 1962, in the Great Leap Forward that left great heaps of corpses in the Chinese countryside. Or maybe forty million—no one knows, because so many people starved that they couldn't be counted. Stalin starved seven million people in 1932 and 1933, when he and Nikita Khrushchev forced collec-tivization on farms in Ukraine. Or maybe it was eight million. Imperial England let a million Irish people starve in seven years, from 1845 through 1852, in An Gorta Mor, the Hunger Great, the potato famine that wiped out an ancient Irish culture and emptied the island.

What might those millions of people have done with enough food and time to dream? What music might they have made, what stories told, songs sung? What miracles were lost, what vast holi-ness, what powerful prayers, what genius children unmade who might have sung the world sweeter?

You never know.

*

I visit writing classes at the university where I work, and I visit high school and grade school classes too, to talk about writing, on the theory that my visit and muttered mumbled guttural nasal rambling is irrefutable proof that a Writer is an utterly normal creature, not especially prepossessing or impressive, a being very much like themselves, except that he carries always two pens, a prime pen and a backup in case of emergencies, and scribble-scraps of paper drift from his pockets like fat snow whenever he excitedly yanks out his first or second pen.

I don't have a stump speech, exactly, when I talk to students, but I have favorite themes, and I hammer away at these as I once hammered away on my younger brothers before they became bigger than me and I sensibly went off to college. In no order these themes are as follows:

Writers are enormously curious. And they are alert to facts and details as merely the visible ends of long invisible stories—bright floats tethered to usually far more interesting matters underwater. A man comes into my office to hang a crucifix. Where did it come from? Who made it? Who carved the Christ, hammered him to the cross? Where did the wood grow? My son for some months sleeps with a can of anchovies under his right cheek; he likes the color of the can. Who packed the anchovies and chose the color of the can? What *are* anchovies anyway? Where do they live, what do they eat, what is the flavor of their lives? My small son loses his small doll's right arm and I find it in a blue jay's nest. There is a story. A cat kills a bird on our lawn and my children conduct a funeral service; I find them praying not for the soul of the bird but for the death of the cat. There is a story. A friend referees a basketball game between two teams of deaf players. There is a story. I attend a basketball game with two blind friends who can tell who is winning by the sound of the sneakers. There is a story. In a small seaside town where I once lived a goose is arrested at the corner of Summer Street and Winter Street. There is a story. With vengeance in my heart I take my first car, a haunted evil thing, to the car crusher and become absorbed with car crushing, which turns out to be a fascinating and peculiarly American corner of life, fully as dramatic and colorful and funny and sad as any movie, and far more entertaining and enlightening. I follow the thread of that story for a while, asking questions, sifting facts like a man with a prospector's pan, and at the other end of the thread I find a huge garrulous storyteller with one eye who is himself of course a riveting and wonderful story. As are we all.

Writers are scribblers, doodlers, scrawlers. "I take a line out for a walk," said the essayist Joseph Epstein, quoting the painter Paul Klee (a creative double play), both trying somehow to explain their creative urge. My father says that the entire difference between writers and nonwriters is that writers get out of bed or out of the shower to write down the great ideas that everyone has in bed or in the shower. Some writers keep journals and diaries and daybooks and quote books, and some carry notebooks with them. I fill my pockets with scribbled-on scraps of newspaper, magazine paper, book endpapers, envelopes, letters, catalogs, bills, my daughter's spelling homework. One essay of mine, about building children's beds, began on a dollar bill.

Writers are wordheads. Writers, good or bad, love words and sentences: their sound, shape, music, appearance on the page, degree of difficulty, everything—"the choiceness of the phrases, the round and clean composition of the sentence, the sweet falling of clauses," wrote the essayist Francis Bacon. Writers are word drunkards, sentence savorers, sentence savers. It's a prerequisite, this lust for language—"a semi-opaque medium whose colors and connotations can be worked into a supernatural, supermimetic bliss," as John Updike has written (beautifully). Language is mostly useless for expressing the tumultuous and terrific emotions roiling us; it is, said Gustave Flaubert, "like a cracked kettle on which we beat out tunes for bears to dance to, when all the time we are longing to move the stars to pity"—yet writers, more than other folk, like to keep trying to move the stars to pity.

I don't say that writers are more sensitive or alert to the infinite shades of the infinite miracles in which we swim; they're not. Children and saints and musicians are most alert. Writers are more diligent about telling stories about the miracles—although "certain it is that words, as a Tartar's bow, do shoot back upon the understanding of the wisest, and mightily entangle and pervert the judgment," as Francis Bacon wrote in a less sanguine moment.

*

But writing is only one of a billion ways to channel and focus a creative itch, and as I age I become ever more alert to the creativity of those who do not produce a commodity, a product, a tangible document of their urge—a play, an essay, a film, a song, a painting, a dance, a meal, a house, a carving, a tapestry. Mothers shape love and macaroni and sleeplessness and soap into young men and women over the course of many years; is there a greater art, or a more powerful patient creativity, than *that?* Teachers shape energy and curiosity and chaos and kindness and order into what we easily and thoughtlessly call *education,* but what is education but a thin word for a long dense creative experience? Priests shape prayer and loneliness and discipline into an hourly courage difficult to even imagine. Politicians are creative not so much in their venality, which fills the newspapers, but in their effort to meld their ambition for power and influence with a desire to serve the murky collective will of defiantly individual voters. Lawyers are creative in bringing language and memory and history to bear against a present danger—be it person or profit margin.

I watched a heart operation once, on a live video feed from an adjoining room, and I was stunned to discover that it was a creative act—that while the surgeon knew the general nature of the problem (a failing mitral valve), the manner of its solution was decided upon on the run, as it were. Indeed the surgeon made a mistake, or miscalculation, during the operation and had to change direction because of it. The man next to me, a surgeon from Australia watching with the furrowed concentration of a hawk, told me that such a thing wasn't unusual, that a great part of a surgeon's skill was the ability to create an operation as you went along, to change direction based on the changing nature of the problem being revealed, to be loosely astute rather than rigidly prepared.

Sport fascinates us for this very reason, I think—for the grace-ful creativity under duress. We are interested in the perfect body, the human creature at its most physically graceful and powerful, a Wilt Chamberlain or Shaquille O'Neal, but we reserve our great-est admiration for he or she who is most creative under the great-est odds, he or she who is calm and intuitive and prepared and loosely astute enough, physically and emotionally, to score the key point, make the crucial catch, wreak the requisite havoc, defuse and defeat the havoc wreaked by others.

*

Writers, interestingly, have never been especially articulate or wise about why they do what they do, and there is a small moun-tain of mediocre to bad books by writers about writing. Generally writers stumble and mumble like the rest of us when asked why we commit creative acts. But there are some pithy remarks here and there that shed light obliquely.

The great science-fiction writer Harlan Ellison was of the benign neurosis school: "I write only because I cannot stop," he said, adding that "anyone can *become* a writer, . . . the trick, the secret, is to *stay* a writer—to produce a body of work that you hope improves and changes with time and the accumulation of skill. To stay a writer day after year after story." There's the very honest school of writing-as-a-good-way-to-pretend-some-semblance-of-sense, starring the novelist Kurt Vonnegut ("Writing allows mediocre people who are patient and industrious to revise their stupidity, to edit themselves into intelligence"), who remains in my memory as the man who characterized Indianapolis as 364 days of miniature golf and then the Indy 500.

There's the writing-as-catharsis school, in which we find E. M. Forster and the novelist Mario Vargas Llosa ("The writer is an exorcist of his own demons"), and the school that says writing is a way to use yourself as a tool to say true things, in which we find

John Cheever ("I write to try to make sense of myself"), Wallace Stegner ("You can take something that is important to you, something you have brooded about, and you try to see it as clearly as you can, and to fix it in a transferable equivalent. All you want in the finished print is the clean statement of the lens, which is yourself, on the subject that has been absorbing your attention. If you have done it right, it's true"), and that tart and direct essayist, the former Saul of Tarsus, who wrote to the Philippians that "whatsoever things are honest, whatsoever things are just, whatsoever things are pure, whatsoever things are lovely, whatsoever things are of good report; if there be any virtue, and if there be any praise, think on these things."

The fine poet Stanley Elkin considered writing a craft ("a kind of whittling, a honing to the bone, chipping away at the rock until you find the nose"), and the fiction writer Kim Edwards has called it something of a magical effort—"more alchemy than logic." Robert Louis Stevenson, whom I believe to be the finest writer to date in the English language, didn't believe that writing was magical, exactly (like Anthony Trollope, he wrote thousands of words a day, often in his sickbed), but he did believe that much of the impetus was inexplicable: "Unconscious thought, there is the only method," he wrote to a friend. "Macerate your subject, let it boil slow, then take the lid off and look in—and there your stuff is, good or bad."

Stevenson knew whereof he spoke; his novel *The Strange Case of Dr. Jekyll and Mr. Hyde* came to him nearly whole in a "boggy dream," and the first draft of the book was written in a three-day white heat unrelieved by meals or sleep—the same manner in which Jack Kerouac wrote *On the Road* on a continuous roll of Teletype paper in 1951, and the same manner in which Samuel Taylor Coleridge wrote "Kubla Khan" in 1798, fresh from a dream in which a vast poem had appeared to him whole, before he "was unfortunately called out by a person on business from Porlock, and detained by him above an hour, and on his return to his room,

found, to his no small surprise and mortification, that though he
still retained some vague and dim recollection of the general pur-
port of the vision, yet all the rest had passed away like the images
on the surface of a stream."

*

I was visiting a class of fourth graders recently, and going on at
tiresome length, as is apparently my habit, about Robert Louis
Stevenson, and how great he was, and how he wrote timeless and
vigorous stuff in every genre, novels and poetry and essays and
travelogues and letters, like a pitcher who could throw the best
curve and the best slider and the best changeup and the best head-
high heater, and a girl in the third row raised her hand to ask an
honest question:

"If Stevenson is the best ever, and you say you'll never be as
good as him, why do you write?"

She had me there for a moment—what do I say? Catharsis? Or
benign neurosis? Or prayer? Or it's an irrepressible gene from my
storyteller ancestors, *seanachaí*, in County Wicklow? Or to stay
sane? Or to make some sense of the world? Or to detect God's
fingerprints?

But then I remembered a line from Samuel Johnson—not a
great writer himself, but the subject of a great writer, James
Boswell, who in his creative biography of his friend wrote a book
about friendship and love and loss that will last for many centuries. Johnson, as Boswell noted, had a soft place in his capacious
heart for his fellow scribblers and would not hear ill spoken of
them, despite the fact that he himself called them "the drudges of
the pen" and noted that "they seldom have any claim to the trade
of writing but that they have tried some other without success." In
fact the Doctor, a prolific if pedantic writer, naturally unburdened
himself of an essay on the subject, titled "Worth of Petty Writers."

This piece concludes with a litany of reasons why newspaper writers, obituarists, gossip columnists, encyclopedists, "abridgers, compilers, and translators" should be appreciated, if not praised.

"Every size of readers requires a genius of corresponding capacity," wrote the Doctor. "Some minds are overpowered by splendor of sentiment, as some eyes are offended by a glaring light. Such will gladly contemplate an author in humble imitation, as we look without pain upon the sun in the water. *Every writer has his use . . .*"

This last was the line that occurred to me as I stood there silent before the fourth graders of Holy Redeemer School, and it is the line I live by as a writer. Many times, most times, my essays are not the finely turned works I wanted them to be. Sometimes they are good enough to convey my point, and in them are several shapely sentences, and some humor, and a witty sally or two, and some novel points to provoke thought. Yet I can count on one hand the essays of mine that I think perfectly wrought, and my ambition as a maker of perfect essays is modest: I'd like to use both hands before I die.

Yet every writer has his use, as the Doctor says, and I have mine. My job—my itch, urge, dream, hobby, entertainment, prayer—is to tell stories on paper, to try to choose and tell stories that both inform and move their readers, and that is what I do to shoulder the universe forward two inches. I was given the urge, and a little of the requisite skill, and I have to do it. It's what I do, and what I love to do, and no one else can do it quite like I do.

Better, perhaps—but not with my peculiar flavor and music, and somehow, in a way I do not wholly understand, that is important, and in a very real sense miraculous, and necessary.

I believe this is true of all of us, every one of us.

A small boy once asked the writer John Steinbeck what he was searching for, as Steinbeck and his friend Ed Ricketts went through a tide pool looking for small marine creatures.

"We search for something that will seem like truth to us; we search for understanding; we search for that principle which keys us deeply into the pattern of all life; we search for the relations of things, one to another," answered Steinbeck.

A good answer. That is why I write.

part one

I Believe

I believe that there is a mysterious and graceful and miraculous Coherence stitched through this world . . .

Room Eight

Every Sunday afternoon I drive seven miles to Room Eight and there conduct the second-grade class in Catholic education. There are fourteen children in my class, ranging in age from seven to nine and in mental age from three to Methuselah. One boy has never spoken, one boy never quite ceases to speak, one girl speaks for her blushing sister, one girl spends all her time staring longingly out the window, and the rest are motley and entertaining novels in the process of being written.

Each Sunday's lesson is supposed to be about something or other but without fail turns out to be about their ferocious curiosity and quiet fears and my overwhelming affection and respect for their fresh-baked minds and mostly honest hearts. When I release them at the end of the hour, two by two like braces of birds, they skip and flutter out of the room and merge with their mothers and fathers smiling and hesitant in the hallway and then hurtle away toward Monday. But I sit there, Sunday after Sunday, in the silent classroom, surrounded by maps and a globe and long sticks of chalk, and contemplate these fourteen difficult graces, and consider that some years from now, when I am old or dead and they are my age, *they* will be the Holy Roman Catholic Church—an idea that has lasted some years now but that could go out of business tomorrow if not for the Room Eights of the world, which are bubbling every day of the week.

So these notes on one room.

*

They sit in gaggles by gender, do my students—a table of chortling boys to my left and a table of grinning girls to my right and in the middle a quiet table of those who got there last and so could not find seats with their sexes.

We start with the Calling of the Roll, a ritual that must precede recorded history, and then there is a heartfelt prayer intoned by the Teacher and amened with laughter by the assemblage: "Dear God, please help us not be mudheads for at least ten minutes, and please let Teacher remember that he said he would give us a five-minute break in the playground, and please let us not shout and interrupt and belch loudly so as to make the whole table dissolve into fits of giggles, and please give Teacher the grace to be alert to the real questions being asked here, which are usually silent and in the eyes, and please let Teacher remember that the vanilla wafers we will use to practice receiving first communion are in his jacket pocket, and please fix Teacher's nose with a miracle so everyone can hear him instead of thinking that they are hearing a truck backfire or a dog throwing up"—and then we sail into the lesson.

At the very first meeting of the class Sarah raises her hand and asks if we are going to use the beautifully printed books we have carefully been issued by the cheerful Franciscan brother in charge of religious education for the parish. There is a gleaming special edition for the teacher, with lesson plans and helpful instructions for suitable music and activities with the chapters. The books are earnest and sincere and boring beyond belief. I spent some hours poring over them before the first class and emerged from the experience goggle-eyed and desperate for vice and whiskey.

"Nope," says the Teacher.

"Good," says Sarah. "They're boring. What are we going to use?"

"Questions and answers."

"Like a test?"

"Yep."

"For a whole hour?"

"Yep."

"Every class?"

"Yep."

"So we can ask you anything?"

"Anything at all. And I'll ask you questions. So we'll just talk. And tell stories. And write stories. And here and there I want you to draw pictures. And at the end I want you to sing a song."

Consternation.

"What kind of questions?" asks Taylor. "Questions about Pokémon? If Charmander and Pikachu had a fight, who would win?"

"No Pokémon questions. Questions about real things. Things that scare you, things you really want to know, honest things. I promise to be honest. I'm not your dad, I'm not really a teacher, I'm not a priest. I'm just a guy. But I try to be an honest guy. So ask me anything you want."

Katie raises her hand. Katie is self-assured and a little resentful that she has to spend every Sunday afternoon—in the *spring!*—at this CCD thing, with some hairy old nutcase who sounds like a dog throwing up. So Katie fires the big cannon right off the bat.

"When the priest blesses the wafer, does it turn into Christ's *real* body? And the wine is *really* his blood?"

Teacher sees that he and Toto are not in Kansas anymore.

"Yes, the bread really does turn into his body, and the wine into his blood. It's a miracle. It's magic. It doesn't look any different, or taste any different, and there's no spark when it happens. But yes—it happens. That's what Catholics believe. We're Catholics. Other religions don't believe that happens, and that's okay—it doesn't mean they're donkeys. But we believe a miracle happens. Who can tell me other miracles?"

"Jesus made wine!"

"Jesus died for the weekend and then came back to work!"

"My little brother learned to wipe himself!"

Hysterics.

Katie waits for the hubbub to die down and then drives right to the basket again.

"Do *you* believe that the bread becomes Jesus' body?"

Katie has hard eyes and those eyes are right on Teacher, who is not the world's brightest man but who senses the moment here, ten minutes into the first class. Do or die, Teacher. Three times you will disown me before the cock crows twice.

"Yes, Katie, I do believe. People will tell you that it's hard to understand how that could be, but the truth is that it is impossible to understand—like a universe that never ends, or how to build a bird. No one knows. We just believe it. We believe that miracles happen all the time and that's one of them. And because it happens you can bring Christ inside you, and that is food for your soul. It makes you a little more open to being holy."

Pause.

"You really have vanilla wafers for us?" asks Tim.

*

One week the whole conversation is about love, and after some major giggling and snickering and sniggering we have us a pretty good talk about the infinite shapes of love, among them affection and respect.

"So being polite to Tim is like *loving* him?"

"Yep."

General disgust.

I keep trying to tell them that romance is only a corner of the cloak and they keep coming back to the icky idea that they will someday actually have to kiss someone of the other gender with their *mouths*. ("Or even your *tongue*," says Erin. "My sister says that's what you have to do when you're sixteen. It's like a law.")

I point out that Jesus loved, was in love, loved well and thoroughly, despite his relatively short time on the playing field. He loved Peter and John, Mary Magdalene, Martha, the thieves hanging next to him, lots of people. He was a funky love machine.

"Did he love the guy who stuck him with a spear?"

"Yes."

"Why? How could he love that guy?"

Teacher doesn't actually know how Christ could forgive a guy who stabbed him with a spear sharp as a razor slicing through his belly as if his skin were warm butter and out poured blood and water, and *he who saw it has borne witness—his testimony is true*, I can hear the next line of John's Gospel in my head, *and he knows that he tells the truth—that you also may believe*.

"Because Jesus knew that the soldier wasn't evil."

"Is anyone evil?"

"Yes."

"Was Hitler evil?"

"Yes."

"Could Jesus forgive him?"

"Yes."

"How?"

I see the savage little Austrian housepainter with his insane eyes, and his mounds of gleaming skulls at Auschwitz, and his mountains of frozen dead at Stalingrad, and I don't know how Christ forgave Hitler.

"I don't know."

"Does anyone know?"

"No. Let me put it this way—God has more mercy than we have sins to commit. He has more aces than we do. Even if we are really evil, he'll forgive us."

I tell them about Catherine of Siena, who had long, heated conversations with God about stuff like this, and how God said to her that he had more mercy in his left pants pocket than any sin had in its whole *house*. God's mercy could kick your sin's butt any day of the week and twice on Sunday.

"So," says Taylor, who has Future Scholar of Hermeneutics written all over him, "I could do a sin and God would forgive me right away?" I see his mind turning the idea this way and that, looking at the interesting possibilities.

We get into how you have to *want* to be forgiven, and if you don't want to be forgiven then you have to burn a lot of hours in the forgiveness waiting room, like at the emergency room at the hospital where you have to wait even if you are bleeding, and this leads us to purgatory and then right to hell, and they want to stay in hell because they love gradations and ranks and hard information about causes and consequences, but I want to sprint back to the New Testament, to the place where Jesus says love is the drug, and bend the conversation back to forgiving, which I think is a really important thing for them to learn, but they're all over hell like flies on honey now, and there's no heading them off.

Paige remembers that I keep harping on how they can ask any question, and she pops a Katie: Do *I* believe in hell?

Pause.

Even the guys' table stops farting and drawing bombs.

I am not wholly conversant with the *Catechism of the Catholic Church* as recently updated and issued with fanfare, but I remember pretty clearly that the Church Eternal does indeed believe that those who die with the stain of mortal sin upon their souls descend to a hell of eternal fire. Additionally I remember that the chief torment of hell is eternal separation from the love of God. I read the *Catechism* pretty carefully when I was about their age and a surprising amount stayed with me even in my hoariness. I dice the question fine in my mind. I could go with the separation from the love of God thread, or I could lean on the reassuring stone wall of Mother Church, or I could answer the question that Paige actually asked, which is about what Teacher thinks.

I don't believe in hell with a capital *H*, I say. I believe in hells but not in Hell. I believe that there are hells on earth, all different kinds, some of them in your mind, but in the hell with flames and manure forks? Nope. I believe my funky boy Jesus when he said love is the drug. I believe that God was telling no lies about mercy when he flapped gums with Catherine of Siena.

"What about Hitler?" asks Christian, who hasn't spoken in three weeks.

"God forgives Hitler," I say with authority.

Then we take a playground break, and I stand there by the swings thinking about Hitler. Hitler was eight years old once, a scrawny little boy swinging on swings, sitting in a classroom chewing a pencil, farting and drawing bombs. I try to form a prayer in my mouth for the icy little killer, for peace on his shrieking tormented soul, but I can't do it. I keep seeing skulls.

We go back to class.

*

Another week they draw and draw and draw. To get loose they draw Teacher, who tells them they can make him as frightfully ugly as they want—in fact there will be a prize for the most horrifyingly ugly rendition of Teacher. Hilarity. They draw the sound of their mother's voice (flowers, the ocean, a radio, and, interestingly, a lawnmower). They draw the face of the Madonna as they imagine it.

"Madonna on MTV?"

"No—*the* Madonna. The real one."

Finally they draw the body of Christ.

Teacher takes these drawings home and studies them late at night, after Teacher's wife and children are asleep. There are several little circles with crosses on them, and two drawings of shreds of bread, and four drawings of a man with a flowing robe and a beard and sandals (although Joe has drawn him wearing stylish high-top Nike sneakers, black ones, with a little arrow pointing to the AIR JESUS logo), but then near the end there is a face I'll never forget, drawn by Paul, who sits at the guy table and is as goofy as the next guy, although I have noticed that he never interrupts anyone. Also his papers are neat, his spelling meticulous, his handwriting careful and firm. Interesting dude, Paul.

It is a haunted face, with huge dark haunted sad eyes. There is the slightest hint of a smile, and Paul has carefully drawn wrinkles on the man's forehead and crow's-feet around his eyes. It is the face of a man with the weight of the world on his heart, a man of infinite sadness, an exhausted man in whom humor is still alive, despite a lurking fear deep behind his dark eyes.

It is the most beautiful drawing of Christ I have ever seen.

*

Most weeks I bring along not only my daughter, Lily, who is in the class, but one of her younger twin brothers, usually Joe. He's five years old. Most of the kids in class are eight years old. Joe is exquisitely sensitive to the difference between ages, as is the class.

Usually things are fine. Joe sits quietly at his desk, grinning at me, writing answers to the questions I ask in class (one time he writes MOM in answer to every question), and he flies around the playground as exuberantly as the rest of the class when we take our break; but one day, as the kids are filing past me back into class, dragging their feet as they shuffle from sunlight into the shadowed classroom, Joe runs right into my crotch and grabs my thighs and hangs on for dear life, sobbing. He won't let go either. The kids wait at their desks for me to walk back in. Kayla holds the door.

A minute, two minutes, three minutes. "What's the matter, Joe, what happened? Use your words"—nothing but sobs. "Joe, I have to teach the class, you have to let go of me," nothing. "Did you fall? Are you hurt?" nothing. Another couple of minutes pass and by now the class is squirming. I waddle back into the room and stand there with my son wrapped around my legs and his convulsive tears wetting my pants, so much so that Taylor assays a half-hearted joke that Teacher wet his pants, but no one laughs and they sit there silently, watching.

I am wearing my son, I think.

I know him well enough to know that a crying jag like this means that his feelings are hurt, not his body. His pride is vast and a slash to it stings him deep.

"I don't know what happened out there, and why he's crying, but if someone was mean to him, that's a sin. If you pick on a smaller boy, or tease him because he's not as old and cool as you, that's a sin. Being cruel is a *sin.* Do you understand me?"

Silence.

"A *sin.*"

Silence.

After a while Lily transfers Joe to her legs and they waddle out into the hallway and sit out there holding each other.

Joe won't stop crying no matter what she does, she says.

I check on them every five minutes. Finally, with about ten minutes to go, he stops crying and Lily comes back in, but he stays out in the hallway, won't come back into class. On the way home in the car he won't tell me what happened. At home his mother asks and he won't tell her either. Finally a couple hours later he tells me that one of the boys kept calling him a baby, and telling him that he didn't belong in the class, and that he could never sit at their table, and did he still wear diapers, baby boy?

I don't ask which boy said this and he doesn't tell me.

*

One week I ask them to tell me stories about their families. Katie tells a long story about how her grandfather talked to God all the time. He had visions, she says. He would shake and fall on the floor. It was scary. But he was a good guy and he would tell the kids in the family about his visions. He said God was a good guy. He said God always had *lots* to say and didn't like to be interrupted and didn't much like being asked questions either. Sometimes God would appear to her grandfather in the kitchen and her grandfather would spill things on the floor. Sometimes God would appear to her grandfather when he was in his recliner chair. He died a couple of years ago. He was a good guy.

*

Another week we end up talking for almost the whole hour about why they are scared of the whole first communion thing. I ask them to write down their feelings.

"I am really skarde," writes Joe.

"I am a little nerverse," writes Kayla.

We talk about dressing up in good clothes, which they don't see the point of, exactly.

"It's to make your parents feel good about themselves," says Erin.

We talk about what to do after they actually receive the Host.

"Nele and prae," writes Nick on his paper.

They line up in the middle of the classroom, jostling and jockeying, and we practice again with the vanilla wafers. They all use their hands, I notice. No tongues sticking out for the priest to place the Host in a wet country. They take the wafer, step smartly to the right, eat it carefully, bless themselves in various fashions and at various speeds, dawdle back to their desks.

Nick sneaks back on line for a second wafer, which leads to a discussion about how often you can receive. "Every hour on the hour," says Paige. Up to twice a day, I tell them, and this reminds me of the late great Catholic writer Andre Dubus, who once wrote that having the chance to receive the Eucharist every day and blowing it off was like having the chance to make love to a beautiful woman every day and not doing so. I refrain from telling this story, although I do tell them about how Andre, who had lost his legs in an accident, often received communion by wishing desperately for it, which is the communion of desire, which counts.

"Even though you don't actually eat it?"

"Yep."

"Huh," says Paul. "Now *that's* interesting."

Other questions?

"What if I drop it? Do I ask for another?"

"What if I barf afterward and it comes up again? Is that a sin? Do I have to eat it again if it has barf on it?"

"If you sin, does the Host refuse to go in your mouth?"

"Can you say 'Thanks' instead of 'Amen'?"

Over and over they ask me the same question, in countless shapes: Are you different afterward?

Yes, I tell them, yes, you are, in a way that you can't see. And how many times this will happen to them, I think—being changed in ways they cannot calibrate. The things that are most real and important are never things you can see, I tell them, their faces gaping and eager. The substance of things hoped for. Love and grace.

With five minutes to go I tell them that I want them to learn the first verse of a song and after a minute of amazed hubbub I sing the verse, and then they haltingly sing it, a few of them diligently silent, Katie turning her face sideways so I cannot see her not singing, Sarah singing like Ella Fitzgerald to my amazement, the Conlon twins grinning at my foolishness at *ever* thinking that cool guys like *them* might sing in front of *girls*, ho ho ho, but I see Nick mouthing the words, which gives me courage, and I sing louder:

> *Amazing grace! How sweet the sound*
> *That saved a wretch like me.*
> *I once was lost, but now am found;*
> *Was blind, but now I see.*

We sing it again and I hear Nick singing "that saved a wrench like me," which pleases me inordinately. I explain that it was written by a tough guy who was captain of a slave ship, and during a howling storm he asked God for help and after surviving the storm he figured amazing grace saved his bacon and he got married and holy and wrote songs.

"Cool! A pirate captain!" says Taylor.

I sing it one more time, because the song is my mom's favorite and she's tough and holy. Then I hear the parents in the hallway, the muted bubbling sound of their voices like a far-off storm at sea, and I stop singing and collect their papers and let them go. A couple of the parents smile uncertainly at me from the hallway.

*

On the way home from class one day my daughter asks me why I don't call on her when I know and she knows that she knows the answer and she has her hand up.

"Well, I'm trying to get everyone involved, even the kids who don't say much, like Ben and Christian."

"But that's not fair. If I know the answer, and I raise my hand first, you should call on me. That's fair."

"But I'm trying to be fair to the whole class, to get them *all* talking about the ideas. They're important ideas. My job as the teacher is to make sure everyone has a chance to think and talk about the ideas."

"So to be fair to everyone you are unfair to me?"

Pause.

"Yes."

"That's not fair."

She's right, of course, and I spend the rest of the drive home thinking about the vices of affirmative action.

*

Another time I ask them to write a letter to Jesus, to tell him whatever they want, whatever they really want to say, not what they think I want them to say.

"Ples four geve me," writes Tim, and then he crumples up the paper into a tiny tight little convoluted loose-leaf-paper brain and hides it in his desk. His brother hands it to me dutifully at the end of class when I ask for all papers to be passed to the front. I smooth it out and stare at it and think, *Four geve us all, Lord, for we know not what we do*—or what Tim did either.

*

The last class is in April, three weeks before their first communion. We have the usual practice with the wafers and the grape juice, and as usual there is a grape juice spill on the floor, and teasing for having spilled the Blood, etc. We have the usual five-minute playground break, during which a brief fistfight breaks out near the swinging tire and Kayla thinks she's been stung by a bee but hasn't. We have the usual roaring of the one word that Teacher would like the class to remember if they remember nothing else from this class for the rest of their born days except a vague recollection that once some hairy nutball who never used the book burned a solid hour of their Sunday afternoons when they were eight.

"What's the word I want you to remember?"

"*LOVE!*"

"Can't hear you."

"*LOOOVVVVVE!!*"

And we have us a good talk about not being scared on the actual day of first communion, and we go over the seven sacraments again—what's the one where the bishop blesses the priest's hands? Oh, right, *ordination*; who can spell that? And what's the one where you get to pick a new name? Right, confirmation, very good, Eric—no, Joe, you can't name yourself Joe Spiderman Conlon, you have to pick a saint to emulate. *Emulate*, well, that means to use as a model, to try to be like.

Do you have to die like they did? they ask. Like the saint who was barbecued? Or the one who was shot full of arrows? What about the girl saints? Do you have to be nuns? Or abscesses, as Paige says, the ladies who are the bosses of the nuns who pray all the time? Do you have to wear long blue coats like the statues of the lady saints always have? And hold your hand up that way the statues always do? Can a regular guy be a saint? Can you be a saint if you like Pokémon? Are there saints no one knows about?

Yes, I tell them—in fact there are millions of saints no one knows about. There are saints all over the place. You couldn't throw a rock and not hit a saint.

And etc.

I want, for this last class, to take a few minutes at the very end to tell them that I will miss them fiercely, that I feel honored to have been with them and of them, that their honesty has been a grace and a gift to me, that I suspect I will weep unashamedly when they are gone and I am there alone in Room Eight, with its acre of blackboards and its globe the size of Paul's head, but for some reason the parents are peering and murmuring outside the classroom door a few minutes early, and the parents looming out there throw everything off, so we close up shop.

After making them pass their papers to the front of class and put their chairs legs heavenward on their desks like dead bugs; and giving them each a totally cool Pilot Precise Rolling Ball Pen with an Extra Fine Point, suitable for use on architectural drawings, as a personal gift from Teacher, pens that I hope they will use for only the very best and truest storytelling and recording of miracles as they notice them; and scrawling my e-mail address on the blackboard at Taylor's request ("Do you have a Web site too?"), I let them go, two by two, like braces of birds: Erin and Sarah first, then Christian and Paul, and Kayla and Katie, and Eric and Taylor, and Lily and Nick, and Paige and Ben, and last the Conlon twins, Tim and Joe.

Erin hugs me as she hurries past, and Paul shakes my hand, and Taylor and I touch fists like how the guy who hits a homer does with his teammate waiting at the plate for *his* turn at bat, and then they are gone.

One of the mothers steps shyly into the room and says thanks, and I say thanks too. I say that teaching her daughter has really been a pleasure, that I learned a lot. She says thanks again and I say thanks again and she leaves.

Then I sit by the globe and weep unashamedly.

Joey's Doll's Other Arm

might be in Denmark for all I know, or Delaware, or perhaps, as my daughter surmises, it disappeared, evanesced, disarmed itself one morning—gathered all its armish energy, curled its hand into a fleshy fist, and punched out of this earthly plane. All I know is that one day it was attached to Joey's doll's starboard side and then the next day it wasn't. For a time it drifted around the house, looking eerily like a lost finger, and then it made its way out onto the lawn, where I saw a jay worrying it one morning (a Steller's jay the size of a robin on steroids), and then it vanished.

My wife thinks the jay took it, and that the arm now hangs out of a nest nearby, not unlike the teenage arms hanging lazily out of the battered roaring cars that clatter and roar up my street, arms that come to life and extend fingers at me when I roar at them from my porch. My daughter thinks that one of the foxes from the nearby fir forest took it, and that the arm is now mounted over the foxy fireplace as a sort of trophy. Liam, who is Joey's twin brother, one minute younger, doesn't think about the arm, or at least he doesn't talk about it. But Joey thinks about it all the time.

He asks about it every morning, when I lift him out of his crib. "Arm?" he asks, holding up the doll to show me its gaping armpit.

"I don't know where the dolly's arm is, Joey."

"Dolly arm owie."

"Damn right, Joey. Dolly sans extremity. Dolly a Democrat—no right wing."

"Owie."

"Yeh, owie. Maybe the arm is out on the grass. Want to look?"

And off goes my oldest son at a gallop toward the glassy front door in search of the grassy arm of his beloved. To no avail. But I admire his persistence, his condensed breath in a circle on the glass of the door every morning, the unflagging relentless drive of his love, and it is that ferocious affection that I wish to reflect on this morning, only a few minutes after Joey galumphed out of the room, his sneakers hammering the beat of his desire on the old oak floor.

All my life I have thought about love, perhaps ever since I was Joey's age and learning then, as he is now, to say, "I love you, Mama" ("Yaiyuffumama," his voice a clear reedy silvery flute), and then through the thunderstorm of pubescent crushes and day-dreams, and then headlong into first serious loves, and then luck-ily, by the grace of whatever gods you wish to summon to this sentence, into married love, which I understand less by the year and savor all the more. And then other rich, broad loves: for my children, an island in the Atlantic, my dearest friends, woodland hawks, the flinty hipbone of the New England forest, the moist matted nap of the Northwest woods. And also, waxing and wan-ing, delightful and puzzling, a love for God. Or god. Or our spiri-tual nature. Or whatever you want to call that occasional overpowering sense of a Sense under and through things.

Often I think we are afraid to speak frankly of God and gods because we cannot read that Mind, because so often religion is evil and greedy and bloody, because faith is so quixotic and unreasonable, because *spirituality* is a word as overloaded with connotation as a log truck top-heavy with the bones of trees. But because we sensibly fear a label does not mean we should be afraid of the content, and I wonder, on this bright morning, if divine love is not unlike Joey's doll's other arm: nearby, sensed, remembered, yearned for, searched for day after day after day, our breaths condensing on the glassy panes of this spectacularly inexplicable world as we look for it.

I also think that this lush troubled world, so ferociously lovely, so plundered and raped and endangered, is *itself* a seething river of divine love, in much the same way as Joey is. Like Joey, the ship of this world came to me from seas unknown; both were made elsewhere and placed in my hands like squirming jewels, and my work and active prayer is to cherish them, to protect them, to try to hear in them the Maker's music, to sing a little of that music myself. Love comes in so many guises, and a deep respect and affection for cedar trees or sockeye salmon is close cousin to a deep respect and affection for children and neighborhoods and wives. Love is a continuum, so a man who says he loves his wife and children is at the least blind and at the most evil if he votes to rape the land (a very slow-moving creature) and kill creatures. He is in a real sense killing his own loved ones; he is killing himself.

The truest words I ever heard about divine love were uttered once by a friend as a grace before a meal. He bowed his head in the guttering candlelight, steam rising from the food before him, the fingers of the cedar outside brushing the window, and said, "We are part of a Mystery we do not understand, and we are grateful."

Agreed. And now to join Joey in searching for it.

The Primary Wish of Your Creator Is Love, Is That Not So?

His Holiness the Fourteenth Dalai Lama, the man considered to be the manifestation of Chenrezig, the Bodhisattva of Compassion, and the leader of millions of Buddhists, and the head of state of a state that is and isn't a state, exactly, has the sloping shoulders of a halfback and the headlong bowlegged shamble of a bear. His gaze is intense and the little hair he has is so short that you want to rub his head as soon as you see him up close, although this is frowned upon by tradition and by the very tall State Department agents who hover near him at all times, the Dalai Lama being the head of a state and all.

The Dalai Lama used to be a boy named Lhamo Dhondup, from the little town of Roaring Tiger in Tibet, but then when he was two years old he was "recognized as the reincarnation of his predecessor," as the Tibetans say carefully, and when he was four years old he assumed the throne of temporal and religious power in his nation. A few years later his nation was gone, eaten by its immense and hungry neighbor, and the boy who used to be Lhamo

Dhondup fled across the mountains to India, and ever since he has been on the road, talking and teaching.

One day his travels brought him to Oregon, where he sat on a cushion at the visitors' end of the basketball court at a Catholic university and addressed an audience of people of every religious stripe imaginable, including a Zoroastrian couple, a gaggle of rabbis, two long rows of priests, an abbot, a dozen nuns, and a man who said he was the head lama of his own sect, which did not yet have any other members, though he had hopes.

Before His Holiness entered the arena proper he was ushered into a holding room at the university, a room where its athletic heroes are enshrined with mammoth wall plaques.

"Who are these famous people?" he asked.

"Football stars, mostly," he was told.

"Ah, America," said His Holiness.

"Too much ideas and ambition make you mad," he said to the president of the Catholic university. "That's why a university with a spiritual context is a very good thing. A warm heart is more important than anything, isn't that so?"

"I couldn't agree more," said the president of the Catholic university.

Once inside the basketball arena His Holiness bowed to everyone in sight and they bowed back, and the crowd stood silent and reverential for a long moment. The absolute silence of thousands of people is a stunning thing. Then he mounted a little platform and folded himself onto his cushion and began to rock back and forth gently for two hours, during which time he talked pretty much continuously, in English for a while and then for a long time in Tibetan, his patient and gentle-voiced translator trying to keep up with His Holiness's thought process, which was quicksilver and ranged far afield.

"Whenever I give a large teaching, I always make clear that it is safer to follow your own traditions, rather than change to another tradition," he said. "There's less confusion. Here in the

West I do not think it advisable to follow Buddhism. Changing religions is not like changing professions. Excitement lessens over the years, and soon you are not excited, and then where are you? Homeless inside yourself.

"I will switch to Tibetan now, thank you. Sometimes when I speak in English, not only do I confuse you, but I have no idea what I am saying.

"Love and compassion are common to all faith traditions. Compassion for all sentient beings made by your Creator, this is integral to Christianity. Christians strive to fulfill the wishes of your Creator, and the primary wish of your Creator is love, is that not so? The Buddha and the Christ were similar men: ascetics, men used to hardship and not to luxury, men of perseverance and effort, extraordinary teachers. And indeed such hardship and ascetic practice are common to all the great spiritual teachers of the world. Yet now we seem to believe that our intellectual progress has advanced us past the great teachers of the past; we seem to believe we are superior to the simple teachers of long ago. But this is a mistake on our part."

At this point a small girl ran up to one of the State Department agents, who bent down from her great height to listen, and then the agent smiled and shook her head no gently and the girl ran back to her seat. The agent said later that the girl had asked if she could speak to the Lama alone now.

His Holiness had a great many other things to say and he said them at great length, even devoting nearly an hour to explicating the single line *All things arise from their causes*, which seemed awfully clear to a number of people in the audience before His Holiness was quite done worrying it to death, but finally the Dalai Lama's two allotted hours in the gym drew to a close and so did his peroration.

"All things are transient," concluded His Holiness suddenly, and there came a great silence. He rocked back and forth on his cushion. "Things change moment to moment, things are impermanent. We worry over the past, we anticipate the future, and we barely perceive a shred of the passing moment. But all of us of every faith tradition possess the possibility of pure light, is that not so? The question of who we are is very much open."

Grace Notes

I s there a richer and stranger idea in the world than grace? Only love, grace's cousin, grace's summer pelt.

*

Etymology: *Grace* is the English translation of the Latin *gratia*, itself a translation of the Greek *charis*, itself a translation of various Hebrew words meaning, variously, love, compassion, fidelity—all used in context of these gifts being utterly free from God to God's creatures. There are no requisites for grace, no magnets for it, no special prayers to lure it. No guru, no method, no teacher, as the Irish genius Van Morrison sings.

You can be good, bad, or indifferent and you are equally liable to have grace hit you in the eye. *Non enim gratia Dei erit ullo modo nisi gratuita fuerit omni modo*, "It will not be the grace of God in any way unless it has been gratuitous in every way," said old Augustine, the grace-obsessed bishop of Hippo, Augustine who considered the whole revolution of his life to be the direct result of a shock of grace. Grace is uncontrollable, arbitrary to our senses, apparently unmerited. It's utterly free, ferociously strong, and about as mysterious a thing as you could imagine.

First rule of grace: grace rules.

*

Grace lifts, it brings to joy. And what, as we age, do we cherish and savor more than joy? Pleasure, power, fame, lust, money—they eventually lose their fastballs, or should: at our best and wisest we just want joy, and when we are filled with grace we see rich thick joy in the simplest of things. Joy everywhere.

Notice how many saints—who we assume were and are crammed to the eyeballs with grace—are celebrated for their childlike simplicity, their capacity to sense divine joy in everything: the daily resurrection of light, the dustiest of sparrows.

*

The undulating grace of horizons and waterlines, of new countries looming up through the mist as the ship nears harbor. The graceful lines of land fleeing in every direction from where you stand in the furrowed field. The smooth sweet swelling grace of a woman with child, the muscular grace of a man's knotted back at work. The cheek of child, the shank of youth, the measured grace of the aged.

The thin brave knobby-kneed yellow sticks that prop up herons, my wife's elegant neck when she folds back her hair with that unconscious practiced female flip of fingers, the slow pained kneeling of an old woman in chapel. The lope of an animal loping. A tree leaping very slowly sunward. A child's hilarity. The endurance of sadness. The shudder of calm after rage.

The bone of the character of a priest who walks to his breakfast with blood on his shoes, the blood of a student who died in his arms in the night after a drunken wreck; the priest is a wreck himself this bright awful dawn, minutes after he blessed the body, but he puts one foot in front of the other and walks into a normal day because he is brave enough to keep living, and wise enough to know he has no choice, and he knows he received grace from the hand of the Lord when he needed it most, first when the boy terrified of dying grabbed him by the collar and begged to be told he would live forever and now, here, in the crack of a morning in a campus parking lot as he hesitates by his car, exhausted, rooted.

But he walks.

*

God grant me the grace of a normal day, prays my wife.

*

What would an alphabet of grace include? Acrobatic, blessed, calm, dignified, ecstatic, eternal, epiphanous, flowing, gentle, harmless, inexplicable, joyous, keen, lissome, momentous, near, oblique, opaque, peaceful, quiet, roomy, salvific, tireless, unbelievable, various, xpeditious, yearning, zestful.

*

Grace in the Old Testament is overwhelmingly a visual affair, from its first mention, in Genesis, where Noah finds grace in the eyes of the Lord, to its last, when the Lord remarks to Zechariah that he will pour grace on the house of David, which will then be able to see "me whom they have pierced"—an evocative foretelling of the Christ. Grace is found "in the eyes of the Lord," "in thy sight," "in your eyes," until one sees that the ancient people's sense of grace was favor, and that they were constantly checking to see if they were on the good side of the One Who May Not Be Named. A crowd of the most interesting characters in the Old Book asks anxiously after grace: Joseph and Moses, Gideon and the sons of Gad and the sons of Reuben, Ruth and Hannah, David and Joab, Ziba and Ezra.

Only in the psalms and proverbs does grace open up and become something poured into lips and into the body, something to be granted to the lowly: "Surely he scorneth the scorners: but he giveth grace unto the lowly."

*

In the New Testament the Christ is grace personified—"the grace of God was upon him," according to Luke, and he is "full of grace and truth," says John, who makes a clear distinction between the prophets and the Messiah: "the law was given by Moses, but grace and truth came by Jesus Christ." The apostles in their Acts are infused and suffused with (and confused by) grace granted them by God, and they thrash out into the country from Jerusalem teaching and preaching and wrestling awkwardly with their newfound power. Those who were not patient are now patient; those who could not preach were now "speaking boldly in the Lord, which gave testimony unto the word of his grace"; those who were shy and clumsy are now "granted signs and wonders to be done by their hands."

That most interesting man Paul has the most interesting things to say about grace. He wants to "testify the gospel of the grace of God," he says to the Ephesians in his last meeting with them, commending them finally "to God, and to the word of his grace, which is able to build you up, and to give you an inheritance among all them which are sanctified." In one of his densest and most eloquent essays, to the Romans, he notes that faith is the avenue to grace, which saves the soul—"access by faith into this grace . . . in hope of the glory of God," as he says. To the Romans he also insists that grace is utterly gratuitous, unearnable: "If by grace, then is it no more of works: otherwise grace is no more grace." He bares all to the Corinthians, and tells them that "lest I should be exalted . . . there was given to me a thorn in the flesh, the messenger of Satan to buffet me," and that "for this thing I besought the Lord thrice, that it might depart from me. And he said unto me, My grace is sufficient for thee: for my strength is made perfect in weakness."

Grace sufficient for the size of your despair, neither more nor less grace than you need!

"Unto every one of us is given grace according to the measure of the gift," says Paul, mysteriously; "God resisteth the proud, and giveth grace to the humble," says Peter, unmysteriously.

The final line of the New Testament speaks of grace, John ending the account of his visions on the island of Patmos with a blessing that has come down familiarly to our time and has many times been spoken over the bowed heads of the faithful, in a thousand languages: "The grace of our Lord Jesus Christ be with you all. Amen." Thus Scripture ends with grace on its lips.

*

Can grace be granted all men, all women, all faiths, all nations, whether or not they have the word of God in their mouths and hearts? O yes, O yes, the church says—interestingly, has always said, no controversies or wrestling matches or murders over the issue—a miracle. And it has eloquently said it, here and there. Orosius, one of Augustine's many disciples, said that grace was showered upon us all *quotidie per tempora, per dies, per momenta, cunctis et singulis*—"daily through the seasons, through the days, through the moments, to all of us, to every one of us."

*

Each person experiences grace as he or she does human and divine love—which is to say, idiosyncratically, in ways different from all others. So we are all writing essays about grace all the time, in all sorts of languages.

*

Physical grace: a certain easy carriage, an authority of lightness, a liquid quickness or liability to litheness, a disciplined exuberance of the body, an unselfconscious ease, a comfortable residence in the body and world. All cats and women have it. Nearly all vegetative things. Most children, most animals, most trees. Many men. Generally the larger the entity the less the grace; this is why we are agog at grace in the largest athletes and animals; why some people watch professional football; why circuses employ elephants—to wow the populace not so much with size as with unexpected grace in the gargantuan.

I think maybe we are so absorbed and attracted by physical grace because we sense how fleeting it can be, how very many enemies it has.

Graceful creatures: a pine marten racing fast and sure over talus and scree; my wife floating through a road race in summer by a river; one of my sons, twisting in the air as he falls backward from a porch step, landing on his hands and knees and bouncing up again in a single smooth motion and sailing away at top speed, not a cry, not a scratch, my mouth falling open to see a body so quick to sense and react, so blindingly quick to rearrange itself. A body wholly at home in the ocean of quick.

*

"I have always been so sure I was right, that I was being led by God," wrote grace-riveted Dorothy Day (whose mother's name was Grace) in her middle years. "I confidently expected Him to show His will by external events. I looked for some big happening, some unmistakable sign. I disregarded all the little signs. I begin now to see them and with such clearness that I have to beg not to be shown too much, for fear I cannot bear it."

One of the few projects she never finished—she was a ferociously energetic woman, flinty, stubborn, not at all sweet, a perhaps-saint made of bone and glower—was a small book to be called *All Is Grace*. "The title really means 'all things work together for good to those who love God,'" she wrote.

Her favorite saint was another flinty woman obsessed with grace, Catherine of Siena, twenty-fourth of twenty-five children, a woman who received the (Dominican) habit at eighteen and then retired to her room for three years, coming out only for Mass. When she *did* emerge finally she was a dynamo, so respected by the church that Pope Gregory XI granted her the power to absolve those who confessed sins to her. Catherine had visions during which God spoke to her at great length, and God, it turned out, is as grace obsessed as Catherine and Augustine and Thomas and us: "My mercy is incomparably greater than all the sins anyone could commit," he said to Catherine. "This is that sin which is never forgiven, now or ever: the refusal, the scorning, of my mercy. For this offends me more than all the other sins they have committed. So the despair of Judas displeased me more and was a greater insult to my Son than his betrayal had been. My providence will never fail those who want to receive it."

Grace unfailing, inexhaustible, endless.

*

Oceans of grace, fountains of grace, rivers of grace. Water is an apt metaphor for grace; it is such a graceful creature itself, sinuous and ungraspable, the first ingredient of life, the substance that composes, cleanses, rejuvenates us, the sea in which we swim before birth.

*

The idea of grace winds thoroughly through religions. In Judaism, one earns grace: "Holiness is twofold," says the Kabbalah. "At first it is effort, then a gift. If you strive to be holy, you are eventually endowed with holiness. Be persistent in learning how to sanctify what you do. In the end, the Blessed Holy One will guide you on the path that it wishes and impart holiness to you, so that you become holy." In Hinduism: "Make every act an offering to me [God]; regard me as your only protector," says the Bhagavad-Gita. "Remembering me, you shall overcome all difficulties through my grace." In Islam: "Knowledge is possible for creatures via participation in Divine Knowledge, such participation being divine aid to creatures," says the *Wisdom of the Prophets*.

*

There are three fundamental themes in the Christian sense of grace, says the Jesuit theologian Roger Haight: it is "absolutely gratuitous," it is (as those rough saints Paul and Augustine discovered) "healing and sanative," and it is elevating. This last rivets me.

*

Further parse the language of apparitions for hints of the nature of grace. "I pour out a whole ocean of graces upon those souls who approach the fount of mercy on this day [the Sunday after Easter, the Feast of Divine Mercy]. . . . On that day are open all the divine floodgates through which graces flow," said Jesus to a Polish woman in 1933, according to the diary of the woman, Helen Kowalska, later St. Mary Faustina, who coughed herself to death at age thirty-three.

*

Grace, says Augustine, is the only value in life and the truest presage of divine presence.

*

Many graceless arguments about grace over the centuries: the Thomists insisting that not Christ but the Trinity is the cause of grace in the angels and Adam and Eve. The Scotists insisting that all grace is from Christ. Pelagius and Augustine arguing about grace and free will—Pelagius, the fan of free will, losing and being bounced from the church, banned for life, ineligible for the hall of fame. We grin now at the fussy ancient theologians splitting the ends of dry hairs about subjects forever beyond their ken and ours, but people were beheaded over these arguments, dismembered, disemboweled, exiled, impoverished, ruined. Later came the Inquisition, later came the military and economic wars in which people were sliced apart in incredible numbers, all ostensibly in the name of God, a bloody habit that the church supported on and off over the centuries. Every Catholic at some point sighs for the church in which he lives, such a wonderful and cruel entity, such a brilliant and idiotic and lurching-gracelessly-toward-grace enterprise.

I remember the words of Paul to the Corinthians: "The letter killeth, but the spirit giveth life."

*

Karl Rahner's final words on this earth, uttered, it is said, with startling authority and joy for a man minutes from *morte:* "All is grace!"

*

Another graceful ending: that of the great British preacher and writer Monsignor Ronald Knox. Drifting in and out of consciousness, Knox wakes to find a friend by his bedside. The friend asks if Knox would like to have some of the New Testament read to him—an edition that Knox himself has translated from the Greek.

"No," says Knox faintly.

And a few minutes later, even fainter:

"Awfully jolly of you to suggest it, though"—his last words.

*

God loves some of us violently; perhaps that savage love is a form of grace too. To wrench from you every shred of peace and feed you nothing but struggle sandwiches every day of your life—is that the highest form of love? If you have the worst life imaginable and struggle ferociously against it, could it be that your fuel to fight is grace? Or that the measure of your courage against your lot is the mark of your character?

How else to understand raped children, broken and bloodied and murdered children, children with ancient eyes, children who were never children, children who bear the marks of evil to their graves, children torn by evil as I write, as you read? *How else to understand them?* Tell me why they suffered and died, or suffered and did not die but were haunted and twisted all their lives by evil done upon them. Tell me why there have been so many millions of little broken Christs. Tell me.

And no one will tell me, for no one knows, only the inscrutable Lord, who never shows his hole cards. So I wonder if most grace in the world is spoken for by those who need it most, and those the smallest among us, their pain the greatest sin of our age.

*

Not-grace: disgrace, gracelessness. I listen to and read of people telling of the moments when they felt grace arriving, and they use words like *calm, serene, harmony, peace, symmetry.* So grace flows, and the lack of grace—not-grace—is a damming of flow, a jamming of gears, a stick in the spokes.

*

The only saint named for grace: Gratia, a sixteenth-century Dalmatian sailor who one day wanders into a Venetian church and is stunned by the sermon (given by an Augustinian). Gratia joins the order and is sent to a monastery where he becomes a legendary gardener and where miracles of light and water follow him like puppies until the day he dies.

*

When have I been filled with grace? One time above all others, when my son was under ether. He was born with a broken heart, an incomplete heart, part of a heart. Not enough to keep him alive. Twice doctors cut him open and cut into his heart. Twice I waited and raged and chewed my fingers until they bled on the floor. Twice I sat in dark rooms with my wife and friends and savagely ate my skin.

The first operation was terrifying, but it happened so fast and was so necessary and was so soon after the day he was born with a twin brother that we all mother father sister families friends staggered through the days and nights too tired and frightened to do anything but lurch into the next hour.

But by the second operation my son was nearly two years old, a stubborn funny amiable boy with a crooked gunslinger's grin, and when a doctor carried him down the hall, his moon-boy face grinning at me as it receded toward awful pain and possible death, I went somewhere dark that frightens me still. It was a cold black country that I hope to never see again. Yet out of the dark came my wife's hand like a hawk, and I believe, to this hour, that when she touched me I received pure grace. She woke me, saved me, not for the first time, not for the last.

As I finish writing these lines I look up and my heart-healed son runs past the window, covered with mud and jelly.

*

I grow utterly absorbed, as I age, by two things: love, thorough or insufficient, and grace under duress. Only those two. Politics, religion, money, ambition—they fade and are subsumed, consumed, eaten by these two vast and endless subjects: love and grace.

Those are the only things we will take to our graves, the only things that will be on our lips as we die, the only things that will be in our pockets as we walk to the country of the blessed—Tír na nÓg, as it was called by my Irish people before me, the country of the always young, where death has no dominion.

We love or do not love, we love well or badly; our friendships are a form of love, our enmities a form of not-love, missing love, weak love.

And grace under duress: what else is there?

Age and illness hammer us, tragedy and evil hammer us, greed and cupidity hammer us; we hammer ourselves in guilt and fear. What are we but the stories of how we fought against our troubles? What good do we remember of the dead but their humor, their stories, their courage, their selflessness, their grace?

*

"One day I am invested mysteriously with my mother's grace," writes Louise Erdrich in *The Blue Jay's Dance*, a gentle and very honest memoir of the first year of her last child. "I am alone with our children. This has been a no-sleep week for each of them. At four in the morning of the fourth night I haven't slept, I sit down, weeping. I fall into a fifteen-minute coma before the next round begins. It happens to be a long crying bout, nothing wrong physically, just growth, maybe teeth. Who knows? Sometimes babies just cry and cry. Morning drags on, our baby continues to cry. Then, in my office, with her in the crib next to the desk, I break through a level of sleep-deprived frustration so intense I think I'll burst, into a dimension of surprising calm. My hands reach down, trembling with anger, reach toward the needy child, but instead of roughly managing her they close gently as a whisper on her body. As though I am physically enlarged, I draw her to me, breathing deeply. The tension drops away. I am invested with my mother's patience. Her hands have poured it into me. The hours she soothed me and my younger brothers and sisters have passed invisibly into me. The gift has lain within me all my life, like a bird in a nest . . ."

We think of grace arriving like an ambulance, a just-in-time delivery, an invisible divine cavalry cresting a hill of troubles, a bolt of jazz from the glittering horn of the Creator, but maybe it lives in us and is activated by illness of the spirit. Maybe we're loaded with grace. Maybe we're stuffed with the stuff. Maybe it's stitched into our DNA, a fifth ingredient in the deoxyribonucleic-acid soup.

*

Grace at meals, that lovely habit of pausing to thank the Generosity who made the plants and fruits, the beasts of the earth and the birds of the sky and the fish of the sea—"Even the *macaroni?*" asks my daughter, and I say unto her, Yea, even the macaroni, and also the Cheerios, and the cheese crackers, and the gingersnaps, for these foods have sustained her like no others, even ye fruits and plants, of which she has cautiously partaken in nibbles that would mortify a mouse.

An ancient urge, the sigh of thanks at the prospect of food, and certainly a habit predating Christianity, but the peoples of the one God gave that whisper of relief and gratitude a graceful name and made it a custom gentle and handsome.

Each home has its own grace or lack thereof, and the litany of formal and informal prayers at table is endless. As a boy I chanted a grace so old in our family that it often suffered hurried hungry editing into one long word—

BlessusOLordandthesethygiftswhichweareabouttoreceivefromthybou ntythroughChristOurLordAmen

—but as a man graced with small children I ask them to name something for which they are thankful before we further reduce the macaroni population. *For my favorite shirt, for my basketball, for my ballet slippers,* they say, grinning, but sometimes they say *for Mom* or *for kids who are dead,* and I think not for the first or last time that prayers from the smallest people are heard first.

*

Me, I am thankful for food. A moment ago in history my forebears ate dirt and grass and nothing in An Gorta Mor, the Hunger Great, the years when Irish children died so fast they littered the sides of the road and were stacked like wood in every corner of the country. I have never been hungry and God grant that I never will, but there is something in me, some gnawing memory, that I think maybe is the shiver of old starving in my tribe—a shred of fear still hidden in the blood, a horror so strong that it stabbed past death into future generations. I notice that carelessly wasted food makes me so unreasonably angry that I frighten my children and myself when I roar at them over spills and splashes, over their petulant or reckless upsetting of bowls and plates. Their faces go pale and I have to leave the room and stand on the porch under cedars and pray for grace.

*

The greatest of grace scholars was Thomas Aquinas, a vast man in several senses—he was nicknamed the Dumb Ox as a student for his silence and bulk and apparently was gifted with total recall of everything he had ever read, especially the Scriptures, which he committed to memory while imprisoned for two years. It was Thomas, in his massive *Summa Theologica*, who strove to explicate every intricate layer and corner of grace (*gratia actualis ad actum*, grace granted by God for the performance of salutary acts, disappearing when the act concludes; *gratia gratis datae*, the extraordinary grace granted miracle workers, prophets, speakers in tongues, visionaries, priests, nuns, monks; *gratia illuminationis*, grace of the intellect; *gratia inspirationis*, grace of the will; etc., etc.), and his treatise on the subject remains the primary scholarly tome. Three times in the last years of his life Thomas was miraculously lifted into the air in church, and those present heard a voice from the crucifix say, "Thou hast written well of me, Thomas."

*

I ask a group of students from abroad about grace. "*Grazia*," says an Italian girl, "*nel senso spirituale, nel senso fisico*," the same word carrying the double load it does in English. "*Sancteiddrwydd*," says a young Welsh woman, or "*trugaredd*," the latter more like mercy; physical grace would be simply "*gras*." I tell them the Gaelic word for the name Grace: *Gráinne*, which hails from the oldest spoken Irish and is thought to mean, rivetingly, She Who Strikes Fear.

"*Grâce*," says a French boy. *Eun-chong* in Korean, *milost* in Czech, *laun ch* in Chinese, *onchou* in Japanese, *ne'ama elaheiah* in Arabic, my head is spinning happily, the students cheerfully writing or drawing the word for me and trying to explain how the idea feels in their languages, their countries, their hearts.

"*Gracia,*" says a sweet shy Spanish girl. "It means the grace that God's catholic has. God has a power to protect and make full happy to people. It's a benediction of God. It's free."

Washed Clean

The rain is raining all around, it falls on field and tree, it rains on the umbrellas here, and on the ships at sea," wrote Robert Louis Stevenson of the Scottish rain, a century ago. Here in the Far Corner the autumnal rains have begun to spill from the sky, and water sluices over land and people, cleansing both, reminding us that we begin in water, are baptized by water, are composed of water. Water is our cousin and our cousin is back in town, his burbling visit forcing us back inside house and heart, back to a chair by the fire, back to contemplation of the ways of water in the stories of the Son who came to us.

One turns to Matthew's Gospel for close accounting of Christ and the waters of the Jordan—waters poured on his brow by a curious and prickly soul so sure that water was the means of salvation that his name has descended to us as John the Baptist. Christ asks John to baptize him with the running waters of a river, that most relentless of scouring creatures.

41

"I need to be baptized by you, and do you come to *me?*" asks John, savage and rude John, John who has just baptized Pharisees and Sadducees while audibly gritting his teeth and lashing them with his razor tongue in a speech that begins with "You brood of vipers!" and then gets less polite, John of the "garment of camel's hair, and a leather girdle around his waist; and his food was locusts and wild honey," as Matthew reports, ever the careful journalist.

"Let it be so now," says Jesus, equably, "for thus it is fitting for us to fulfill all righteousness." And so on his brow John pours the waters of the Jordan, the mighty river of Judea.

"And when Jesus was baptized," writes Matthew, "he went up immediately from the water, and behold, the heavens were opened and he saw the Spirit of God descending like a dove, and alighting on him; and lo, a voice from heaven, saying, 'This is my beloved Son, with whom I am well pleased.'"

Staring out the window at the gray corduroy sky, one thinks of that stern Voice falling down in praise upon his Son, and suddenly the rafts of rain do not seem onerous but holy, do not seem an affliction but an extraordinary gift; this is the water of life, and we drink from it so that we may live, in him, with him, until the waters part and there is nothing but Light.

part two

Yesuah ben Joseph

Gaunt, skinny, dusty, testy,
patient, impatient, poetic,
mystifying, mysterious, adamant,
frightened, confusing, stunning,
riveting . . .

Joe's Boy

He must have had a crush on a girl and been utterly fumble-fingered and mumble-tongued about the whole thing. He must have punched and in turn been punched. He might have sobbed at a death, sweated in fever, roared at his father, snapped at his mother, embraced them abashed and ashamed. He must have been riveted and puzzled by his own body, such supple and fragile meat. Maybe he ran naked howling laughing through the village on a dare. Maybe he had waaaaaay too much wine at a wedding. Maybe he gnashed his teeth at the incomprehensible stupidity of sheep and maybe he gawked when an eagle the size of a tent flapped past his head and maybe what he wanted above all else like every child ever born was to leap ahead in time and bite into life, except that he already knew his fate, knew it earlier than any child ever should, knew the cold hour of his death and the haunted face of his betrayer; yet I wonder if he wondered what his life would have been like if he'd been born any other boy than the boy he was.

Maybe he wondered about his name, which had come to his mother in a vision before he was born. Maybe he wondered to hear that he had gone nameless for seven days after his birth, and that a devout old man had prophesied over him, and that an old woman in the temple had approached his parents singing thanks for his birth.

Certainly he loved lore and law, for when he was twelve years old his mother and father brought him to the big city, but when his parents started back to their village he slipped away and stayed in the vast temple among the old teachers, and there he asked stunning questions and posed extraordinary answers, to the general amazement of the old teachers, and when his parents returned desperately to find him, and his mother asked, naturally enough, how he had the cool nerve to miss the train home, he answered her with some major sass that he had *real* work to do, and it was all his mother could do to keep her husband from pitching the boy headlong into the manure pile outside the temple.

But she treasured those words in her heart.

From then on, until Tiberius had been emperor fifteen years and Joe's boy was nearly thirty, we hear nothing more of him; the legends say only that he increased in stature and wisdom, which makes it sound like he was eight feet tall and a genius. But he must have been slender, even slight, for he was a tireless walker, and could fast for forty days at a time; and he must have been wiry strong too, for the one time he popped a gasket and lost his temper altogether he tossed tables and moneychangers around like Frisbees in the very temple where he'd given his mother such nervy lip when he was twelve years old.

You know the rest of the story, and a remarkable story it is—maybe the greatest story there ever was. I think so. I think Joe's boy told no lies, and love will save your life, and light and mercy will be our food until the end of time. But if we remember only the legend of this man, and not the skinny intense confusing man himself, we do him disservice and disrespect, for he was once one of us, which is to say he *is* us. That is his message and genius; that is the song he sings still.

JC1654

Some months ago a thin bearded man appeared in my office, propped a ladder against my wall, climbed aloft, and nailed a thin bearded man to the wall. This latter thin man, I should say, is bronze, and six inches tall; he is also wearing a bronze loincloth and a bronze circlet of thorns. The cross to which he was nailed is walnut, fifteen inches long and seven inches wide.

The first man, having hung the second man, departed without a word.

I sat and stared at the small bronze man, and pondered, not for the first time and not for the last, his most unusual life, his cruel death, and his astonishing return—perhaps the most interesting and significant story in the long thousands of years that human beings have told stories of magic and power to one another.

But I also saw, as if for the first time, the crucifix itself, and wondered about this macabre talisman—not so much about its long history as a symbol (some fifteen centuries), or the extraordinary artistic renditions of it (by such geniuses as Velázquez), or its historical inaccuracy (Christ would have been crucified naked, for greater humiliation), but about the fact that it is still being made by human hands some two thousand years after the incident depicted occurred on a dark afternoon in Judea.

I wondered, in short, who made the little Christ in my office, and how did he get here?

He is, I discovered, JC1654, from the Jeweled Cross Company of North Attleboro, Massachusetts, a company named for its very first product, a rhinestone-studded crucifix made at a kitchen table for a wake in 1922. The Jeweled Cross Company, which today makes more than a million religious items a year, cast JC1654 from a mold carved by their in-house sculptor, and milled the cross from walnut grown in Pennsylvania, and cast the tiny bronze sign above the corpus (INRI, *Iesus Nazarenus Rex Iudaeorum*, "Jesus of Nazareth, King of the Jews"), the Roman insult to Jews carefully reproduced in America two thousand years later.

From Massachusetts, JC1654 was sent to a store in Oregon. This store sells church supplies and devotional products, among them some one thousand crucifixes a year of the more than a million sold annually in the United States—numbers easier to digest, perhaps, when you remember that rosaries carry tiny crucifixes, and there are crucifixes for automobile dashboards and holy-water fonts, and crucifixes for key chains, pendants, medals, sick-call sets, pyxes, processions, and altars, among many other uses.

From that store on the main street of a city, JC1654 traveled north four miles, in a van, in the company of forty-nine identical JC1654s, to a carpentry shop at a small Catholic university, where the university's carpenter, a quiet man whose hobby is building altars, hammered the bronze corpus to the walnut cross with brass nails (this is the K-model JC1654, which is designed to be assembled at the place of display). The carpenter hammered the tiny bronze INRI sign into the cross above the corpus too.

Hammering Christ to the cross fifty times took him a long time, he said, because he was trying to be especially meticulous about his work, because walnut is a strong wood not easily pierced, because the infinitesimal brass nails (called "brads") were almighty difficult to handle, because the bronze corpus was fragile, and because the job had an altogether strange cast to it, truth be told.

From the carpenter's shop, JC1654 was carried across campus by the thin bearded man who entered my office one day without a word and hung Christ on the wall above my door.

He's been here for a few months now, has JC1654, and I've developed an affection and a respect for him. He traveled all the way across the country to be here, for one thing. And he rather elevates our room, which otherwise is a thick jungle of papers and books and motley visitors. And he reminds me, every time I glance up from my desk, that once upon a time there was a man who so loved men and women and children that he let himself be beaten and scourged and stabbed and broken, and let himself be nailed to a massive cross with massive nails, and let himself be killed, slowly and with unimaginable pain, so that people he never knew would have the chance to live in the unimaginable love of the Creator of everything we know.

And he reminds me too, every time I look up and catch the dull bronze glint of his sagging body, of all the millions of men and women and children who have given their bodies and lives for others, and give their bodies and lives now, right this minute, so many of them silent in their struggles and never to be celebrated or sainted after their difficult lives and obscure deaths.

None are Christ but all are Christlike; and that, finally, is why I bear such affection and respect for JC1654, for he reminds me to love—and there is no greater law, nor more difficult work, nor deeper joy.

So said the mysterious man depicted on my wall: and I believe him.

Mister Louie

In my Sunday school class there are eleven or twelve children, depending on whether Brendan has a soccer game. From the start we promised to be honest with one another, a vow that has led us on interesting journeys, one of which came just before Christmas, when I asked them to rename Jesus.

"His name is getting in the way," I said. "We are taking him for granted. He's a brand name, an adjective, a label, a myth, a legend. So we will give him a new name and maybe wake him up in our hearts. What's his new handle?"

"Pi," said Brendan, the oldest.

"T. Rex," said Erik.

"Spiro," said Mike.

"The Dude," said Louise.

"Bobby," said Megan.

"Zab," said Danny, the youngest.

"Iggy," said Emily.

"Q," said Werner, who wears a jacket and tie to class.

"Tank," said Elizabeth, startling me; she is the soul of feminine decorum.

"Corky," said Joey, my son.

"Jackie," said Liam, my other son.

"Mister Louie," said Will, after a judicious pause. Will doesn't usually say much, so this was an entertaining bolt from the blue. We tried these names on for a while to see which fit Jesus best. Corky Christ got some votes for the alliteration, and Iggy Christ sounded pretty good, although it sounded like a Yiddish barber to me, and Bobby Christ sounded like a stock-car driver, and The Dude got some votes for its low-slung surfer tone, and Liam had his heart set on Jackie Christ, who sounded like he played second for the Dodgers, but because I am the teacher I got ten votes and I threw my block to Mister Louie, which got thirteen votes and carried the day.

So we have used Mister Louie since as a name for the human incarnation of the Lord of the Star Fields—interchangeably with Jesus, and with Yesuah ben Joseph, his name in Aramaic—and I report that it has worked pretty well. My students spend a lot more time thinking about the peculiarities of Mister Louie's predicament than they did when his name was a name people use when they lose their tempers. They spend more time pondering the nature of his miracles than they did when "Jaysus" was a name they heard rattled off a hundred times in the space of ten minutes on a God channel on cable television. The thin man who changed the world forever and left the most stunning story behind him is a little more real now to these curious children than he was before; and maybe that's everything.

One day we talked about Mister Louie's clothes and family and schooling. Another time we talked about how he might have felt when he healed a blind man with spit and dirt, and prayed desperately for a little dead girl to be alive, and had a sponge with sour bitter vinegar crammed in his mouth by a sneering soldier.

We talked about how you could ask Mister Louie for help when you were crying or scared or so angry you wanted to hit your brother with a basketball *"right between the eyes as hard as you can,"* as Brendan growled.

Finally one day Elizabeth said something so naked and direct about Mister Louie that after she said it I excused myself and walked out of the room and wrote it down.

"It doesn't matter what we call him," she said. "It doesn't matter what his name is really. It just matters that we can still talk to him and that he said love is the boss. Isn't that right?"

Christ's Elbows

L ost, usually, in the awe and mystery of stories of Christ the
Lord of the Star Fields is the sheer coltish *physicalness* of
Christ the wiry young man, in his early thirties, at the peak of his
professional and physical career, before the events that ended his
life suddenly at age thirty-three.

Accounts of his body in action are few and far between. Luke
gives us an early glimpse of the boy Jesus, who "grew and became
strong" and grew "in stature," and we may imagine him hauling
lumber for his stepfather, and straining to curve planks for chairs,
and engaging in the assorted other labors of a carpenter's appren-
tice, not to mention grumbling through the various physical tasks
around the house to which he was set by his mother, who loved
him like crazy but still needed some strong-backed young help
digging in the garden, sweeping the kitchen floor, washing
clothes, etc.

And we may further imagine him in the unaccounted time
between his twelfth year, when he scared his parents half to death

by staying behind in Jerusalem and gabbing with the rabbis in the temple, and his thirtieth, when he entered public life by plunging into the Jordan River and watching his brusque cousin John's hairy arm douse him with baptismal water. Perhaps he ran through the fields for miles at dusk to shake off his restless teenage energy; perhaps he relished competitive fisticuffs with his jumpy energetic friends; perhaps he sprang over high stone walls with the coiled muscularity of a basketball player. For all we know he was a terrific athlete, not at all the polite quiet simpering mama's boy that centuries of devotional painters would have us admire.

But for the most part we have to invent his athleticism, because there is a notable paucity of physical references to Christ in Scripture. This is easily understood; the various authors of the Gospels wished to recount tales of the Christ that would reveal both his unique divinity and his many (fascinatingly phrased) suggestions for right living and eternal salvation. And because the Gospels are not eyewitness accounts but quasi-historical essays very much meant to persuade and convert, they lack an eyewitness's attention to their subject's physical presence: carriage, bearing, bounciness of stride, height, weight, injuries; the strength of his handshake, the length of his fingers (Did his hand swallow the hand of the girl he raised from the dead? Could he palm the heads of the children who followed him like puppies?), the weight of his hand on the shoulders and faces of the men and women he healed with his touch.

So mostly what we see of the physical Christ in the Gospels, until his last herculean hauling of the cross, is the travelin' man—walking, walking, walking, all over Judea, sitting down to teach, getting up to move off when he is done, reclining here and there before a meal, but then up again and out the door and back on the road, go go go—the man was relentless, a preacher with no off button. We might well picture Christ with the thin hard body of a marathon racer, all bones and ropy muscles, considering the miles he racked up in three years; we might also better understand why the washing of feet was such a momentous ritual at the time, especially for Christ, who must have sighed many a night when he stared down at the worn and dusty pins that had carried him so far so fast.

But there is one hour in his recorded life when we see a flash of utter furious physical action on Christ's part, an hour when this most curious of men must have experienced the sheer joyous exuberance of a young mammal in full flight: when he lets himself go and flings over the first moneychanger's table in the temple at Jerusalem, coins flying, doves thrashing into the air, oxen bellowing, sheep yowling, the moneychanger going head over teakettle, all heads turning, *What the . . .?* You don't think Christ got a shot of utter childlike physical *glee* at that moment? Too late to stop now, his rage rushing to his head, his veiny wiry carpenter's-son arms and hard feet milling as he whizzes through the temple overturning tables, smashing birdcages, probably popping a furious moneychanger here and there with a quick left jab or a well-placed Divine Right Elbow to the moneylending teeth, whipping his scourge of cords against the billboard-size flank of an ox, men scrambling to get out of the way, to grab some of the flying coins, to get a punch in on this nutty rube causing all the ruckus . . .

In all this holy rage and chaos, don't you think there was a little absolute boyish mindless physical jittery joy in the guy?

Think of the *man* for a second, not the eternal Son of Light; remember that this most riveting of figures was equally God and man, and then put yourself in his place, halfway through the roiling roaring riot of the temple that day. Things are completely out of hand, utter disorder, and he knows in his heart that there will be hell to pay, so to speak, when he's done tearing the place apart. But he also knows he's right, and that he is fulfilling the prophecy laid out for him ("Zeal for thy house will consume me"), and for once in his careful, marching-toward-eternity-and-salvation-for-all life he's let himself go utterly, he's *not* being careful, he's on a rocking, socking, cathartic roll, he's unstoppable, his elbows are flying like a professional basketball player's; and I bet a buck he was grinning from ear to Christly ear.

And God bless him for it.

The moment would end, of course, and the cops would come, figuratively speaking, and he would have a tense exchange with the men he'd just thrown out of the temple (moderates on each side holding back the combatants as they strained to get in one more blow, the veins in their necks bulging as they yelled at each other), and he would resume the life and work that rivet us to this day. But I smile whenever I think of him wading into the seething mass of prim bankers in the temple and upending their world with a broad grin on his face. So he upends our world, over and over, every single day if we are lucky and attentive, and it is a grace upon us if we smile as our own prim plans for making money and careful living go flying all to pieces.

Perhaps the chaos of our plans is the shadow of his smile.

A Thin Ragged Man

Several months ago a man named Walter appeared at our door. He was a slight ragged man, gaunt, dirty, polite. He worked hard all day in the basement, sheetrocking walls and building a wooden floor. He worked hard all the next day too. The third day he barely worked at all. He spent the day eating sandwiches and talking about himself. He had served three tours in Vietnam, some of them in a psychiatric ward. He said that he had a wife and child but they left him, that someone had recently stolen his truck and tools, that he was grateful for the work in our basement.

On the first day he estimated the cost of his work and we agreed on a price. I bought all the supplies and borrowed tools. On the second day he asked for an advance and got it. On the third day he asked for another advance and got it. He also asked for a raincoat and a ride into the city and got them too. I dropped him off in the city; my daughter and I waved to him as he shuffled off.

That was the last we saw of Walter for a while. I returned the tools. Two weeks later he showed and worked hard all day again.

He said he'd badly underbid the job and asked for another advance. We said no. His face fell. He was out on the streets, he said, and needed to find ten dollars a day for his methadone shot. We said no. He saw my wife's beloved old backpack and sleeping bag and proposed that he finish the job in exchange for them. Okay, said my wife. And Walter walked off into a howling thunderstorm carrying the pack and bag and we never saw him again.

Walter is a thief, a hapless ragged polite thief, a liar, a heroin addict. I hate him. He stole our money, left the basement a shambles, reduced my wife to tears at the waste of money and time. I hate that he held my children, that he shook hands with my wife, that he ever set foot in my home. But if I believe that the gaunt ragged man who died between thieves on the Hill of Skulls was reborn, I have to look for him in Walter. This is very difficult for me.

But as long as love wriggles out of hate there is faith.

*

The preceding essay was first published in Portland Magazine, *the quarterly magazine of the University of Portland, in its spring 1996 issue. A few weeks later I received a letter from Jim Wood, a prisoner at the Eastern Oregon Correctional Institution, who has given permission for his letter to appear with my essay.*

Dear Mr. Doyle,

As a rule I avoid writing people I do not know; but, after reading "A Thin Ragged Man" in *Portland* for Spring of '96, I feel compelled to write you. Please bear with me as I struggle with my emotions and the difficulty of expressing them, along with my thoughts, to a person who is a stranger to myself and my experiences.

Why do I feel so compelled to write you? Because I believe that you want to follow God's instruction and Christ's example to love and to forgive, from that love, those who trespass against you. I believe that I know enough about Walter to help you, for I am a man much like him.

When I read "A Thin Ragged Man," I felt an immediate pull, a connection with all of you. You see, Mr. Doyle, I am an addict like Walter. I have struggled even in the deepest, most desperate times to throw off the chains of addiction, only to fail. I, like Walter, have tried to salvage sanity and my humanity through honest labor and reaching out for some connection to "normal" people, only to fail because of my own feelings of inadequacy, shame, and apartness. Please believe, Mr. Doyle, I am not writing you to complain about my life. I believe that you truly meant what you said, "As long as love wriggles out of hate there is faith." I believe you hate Walter right now. I believe that you don't want to do so. I also believe that love grows from knowledge, understanding, and (mostly) empathy. So, please, let me tell you about Walter.

Walter, too, hates the life he lives. He knows what he has become—"a hapless, ragged, polite thief, a liar, a heroin addict"— and every day he curses the self-made choices that brought him to that point in life; and because those choices were self-made, he hates himself. Can you imagine the shame he felt sitting in your house? This man wanted to work honestly to support himself, maybe even to begin the slow march back. Knowing all that Walter has lost over the years—spiritual strength, family, home, self-respect, dignity, ad infinitum—it is not hard for me to feel the terrible ache, emptiness, and shame that he felt.

You see, Mr. Doyle, every moment that he was in your home, Walter compared himself to you. He saw not what you have but what he has lost, and it tore him apart. Walter had probably just gotten "clean"; otherwise, he could not have worked diligently for a half-day, let alone two full days, in your basement. Can you imagine the turmoil Walter was in without the warm, numbing, emotion-dampening blanket of heroin and much experience in dealing with real emotions? He may not have had adequate experience in dealing with them, but he sure knew how to kill the pain and the shame; hence the "advances."

The lie Walter told himself was that he could leave that second day, numb his pain with "just one," and be all right. Imagine the added shame as it sunk in the next day as he sat in your home relating to you all, while he tried to work up the courage to ask for another advance, just how impossible it was to do "just one." Imagine also that Walter knows that he has disappointed and hurt you; he does, and it is one more ache that he will use to beat himself emotionally. Do not believe that Walter came to your family's home to con you or to steal from you. The fact that he is hated for his actions is evidence that he took from you emotionally as well as financially.

This letter is *not* for Walter's benefit. He and his life will improve only through much clean time, appropriate treatment, and God's grace. I pray that he either gets into detox or gets arrested to begin the journey. This letter is for you and your family. If you must hate, hate the behavior, not the man. Understand that as poor, ragged, and hapless a thief as Walter is, he is a man who truly wants not to be as he is. Pray that your wife's "beloved old backpack and sleeping bag" are keeping him warm and carrying his few possessions safely. Someday he may forgive himself and he will seek to make amends. Love the man and Christ will shine forth through you.

For now, please allow me to apologize to you for Walter. I know that he wants to himself. Mr. Doyle, God bless you and your family.

Sincerely,
Jim Wood

part three

A Catholic Being

I believe that everything
is a prayer . . .

Credo

Recently a friend asked me why I am Catholic. I mumbled the first few reasons that entered my head—the faith of my family, the enticing power of the story, an increasing belief as I age that divinity indeed infuses all things and that Christ, dead in the dust at age thirty-three, was indeed distilled divinity.

My friend was satisfied and moved the conversation along to other things, but I was not satisfied and so have continued to write down reasons that I am Catholic:

I believe that a carpenter's son named Jesus indeed cracked time in half, entered this world in the guise of a squalling infant, said his piece, was slaughtered for his pains, and cracked time again on his way home. I have no real basis for this belief, and neither do you. We either believe the man or we do not, and I do, for reasons I know and do not know.

Some of those reasons I can articulate. I was born into a Catholic family, and early learned to love the smoke and poetry and incantation of the Roman rite. My friends were Catholic, and we were as bound by our common faith as we were by our exuberant youth, European forebears, and itchy masculinity. Catholicism was the faith of my Gaelic forebears, whom I greatly respect in absentia. It was the faith of my grandmother, who shriveled and died before my eyes when I was twelve years old, and whose funeral Mass taught me the enormous power of ritual, the skeleton that sustains us when we are weak. And Catholicism was the faith of my alma mater, where I stuttered into manhood, and of three of my professional employers.

But I believe in Christ for muddier reasons. Sometimes I desperately need to lean on a god wiser and gentler than myself. Sometimes I desperately need to believe that when I die I will not be sentenced to Fimbul, the hell winter, where there is only the cold voice of Nothing, but rather I will be at peace and draped in Light. Sometimes I am nudged toward belief by the incredible persistence and eerie genius of the tale: the encompassing love of the mother, the wordless strength of the Father, the Lord of All Worlds cast ashore on this one as a mewling child in dirty straw. Sometimes I am moved past reason by the muscular poetry and subtle magic of these stories. Sometimes it is an intuitive yes as the light fails and the world is lit from below. And sometimes I simply cast my lot with the sheer bravura of such a patently brazen lie. That a man could die and live again is ridiculous; even a child knows that death is the end.

Or is it?

I do not want to be sure about that. I want to meet my quiet father-in-law, a man I never knew, and thank him for the lovely miracle of his last daughter. I want to meet my brother Jimmy, who died in his carriage on a bright April day in 1947. I want to meet William Blake, Dexter Gordon, Crazy Horse, Robert Louis Stevenson, Rosemary Clooney. I want to kiss my grandmother again on her leathery cheek. I would like to see my friend Dennis Green, age twenty-three, who died on a humid highway in Florida while I was writing these words. I would like to meet this fellow Christ, who haunts the edges of my dreams, who flits from tree to tree in the forest through which I make my way. I would like to live forever, and hold my wife and daughter and twin sons in my arms until the end of time, and daily read the immense poem of Death into Life, and grin at the whirl and swirl of its endless unfolding, until the end of Until.

So I am a Catholic for many reasons. Sometimes I think I might also be a Buddhist, because that faith is calm and wide, and sometimes I think perhaps I am also a pantheist, because I smell divinity in music, herons, drunkards, flowers. But Catholic is my language, Catholic is the coat I wear, Catholic is the house in which I live.

It is a house that needs cleaning, a house in which savagery and cowardice have thrived, where evil has a room with a view, where foolishness and greed have prominent places at the table. But it is also a house where hope lives, and hope is the greatest of mercies, the most enduring of gifts, the most nutritious of foods. Hope is what we drink from the odd story of the carpenter's odd stepson. When we eat his body in the ludicrous miracle of the Mass, we hope in him, and with him, forever and ever, world without end, amen, amen, amen.

Altar Boy

I will go to the altar of God,
to God my exceeding joy.
—Psalm 43:4

Introit
I missed one Mass as an altar boy—the Tuesday dawn patrol, 6:00 A.M., Father Dennis Whelan presiding. He was a good-natured fellow, a cigar smoker although he was a little young for it, that kind of guy, but he was furious when I trudged back to the sacristy after sitting through the second half of Mass in the very last pew.

Where were you?

I was late, Father.

You miss another and you're out of the corps.

I'm very sorry, Father.

It's no joke to be all alone out there.

Yes, Father.

I knew why he was peeved; I was the key to his famous twenty-two-minute Mass. He pulled off this miracle week after week, without ever looking at his watch. His Mass drew the faithful by the dozens, especially businessmen trying to catch the weekday 6:30 train into New York City. One time Whelan had the 6:00 on St. Patrick's Day and we had nearly fifty people in the church—still a record for our parish, I bet.

Working with Whelan was a pleasure; he was a real artist, someone who would have made his mark in any field. He had all the tools—good hands, nimble feet, a sense of drama, a healthy ego, the unnerving itch to be loved that all great performers have. He did not rush his movements, mumble, or edit his work. He was *efficient*, yes—he'd send his right hand out for the chalice as his left was carving a blessing in the air, that sort of thing—but every motion was cleanly executed and held in the air for the proper instant, and he had astounding footwork for such a slab of meat. He was one or two inches over six feet tall, 250 pounds maybe, big belly sliding around in his shirt, but he was deft on the altar and could turn on a dime in the thick red carpet. He cut a memorable double pivot around the corners of the altar table on his way to his spot, and he cut that sucker as cleanly as a professional skater before a Russian judge.

My job was simple: I was the wizard's boy, and the whole essence of being a great altar boy was to be where you needed to be without seeming to get there. Great altar boys flowed to their spots, osmosed from place to place. They just appeared suddenly at the priest's elbow and then slid away liquidly like Cheshire cats. There were other arts—quick work with the hands, proper bell ringing, a firm hand with matches and candles, the ability to project a sort of blue-collar holiness on the stage, that sort of thing—but the flowing around like a five-foot-tall column of water was the main thing, and it was damned hard to learn. Rookies spent their whole first year, and often two, lurching around the altar like zombies, a tick behind Father's moves, which led to, horror of horrors, an irritated Father gesturing distractedly for what he needed. Extra gestures from the wizard were the greatest sins, and we recoiled in horror when we saw them when we were at Mass with our families and out of uniform. At such moments, when the clod on the altar forgot to ring the bells, or brought the wrong cruet, or knelt there like a stone when he should have been liquiding around the altar in a flutter of surplice sleeves, I closed my eyes in shame and in memory, for my rookie year was a litany of errors too long to list, and my graduation from rookie to veteran was a source of great pride to me.

Gloria
Whelan was all business out there from the moment he strode purposefully through the little doorway from the sacristy. He had to duck a bit to get under the lintel easily, but even this little dip was done smoothly and powerfully, as if he had trained for it. This quick duck-and-rise move made it appear that he was leaping onto the stage, and he always startled the railbirds getting in a last ask before the lights went up; by the time Whelan was front and center, the old birds were back in their pews doing the rosary ramble.

Whelan ran his Mass like clockwork, and God help the boy who was still sleepy, because the man knew our marks like they were chalked on the floor, and he expected us to be quick with the equipment of the Mass—glassware, towels, smoke. Cruets were to be filled to the neck, incense respectfully removed from the boat and properly lit in the thurible, hand towel clean and folded over the left arm, Mass book open to the right page, bells rung sharply at exactly the instant he paused for the sharp ringing of the bells. He also liked his wine cut with water in advance, half and half. Most priests liked to mix it themselves during Mass. Some drank mostly water with only a touch of wine for color and legitimacy; some drank the wine straight, with barely a drop of water. Few priests drank a full load of wine; even the heavy hitters found cheap Burgundy distasteful at dawn. We did too, although there were more than a few boys who drank wine in the musty stockroom, and every altar boy at some point gobbled a handful of communion wafers to see how they tasted fresh from the box. They tasted like typing paper. After I discovered that the Hosts came wholesale from a convent in New Jersey, the consecrated Host never tasted quite as savory again.

Oremus

I joined the altar boys because my older brother was in the corps and because my parents expected it. Also you could get out of class for funerals. Funerals didn't pay anything but weddings did, usually a buck, although there were rumors of five-dollar weddings, and it was said of one boy that he had once received a twenty-dollar bill from a bride's father who was drunk. Baptisms didn't pay—a quarter, maybe, if you were doing twins. The way to make money was to work the banks of candles on either side of the altar. The big ones were on the left and the little ones were on the right—"Big ones for the horses and little ones for the dogs," as Mr. Torrens, the altar master, said with an enigmatic smile. He was a horseplayer, I think.

People would come up to the candles before and after Mass, and if you were there in uniform they'd hand you the money, even though the steel box was right in front of them. Large candles were a dollar and small ones were a quarter.

Light a big one for my grandmother, they'd say, crumpling a bill into your hand.

Here's a quarter for my boy at sea.

Here's a quarter for a marriage.

A quarter for the pope's health.

Two smalls, for my intentions.

A dollar for the dead.

The code among us was that coins placed in your hand were yours; bills went into the box. The theory was that we were just standing there, and the women (they were mostly women) were handing us money out of the goodness of their hearts. This was the first tickle of sin for some of us, and while the practice enriched some boys, it was by no means universal, partly because our cassocks had no pockets and partly because Mr. Torrens learned about it from a first-year boy and after that kept a sharp eye on us from the sacristy door. A boy named Frank Rizzo was asked to leave the corps because of this and it caused great embarrassment to his family. He became a bully in adolescence and probably still is.

The Poem of the Twenty-Two Rites and Thirteen Masses
When I was an altar boy there were twenty-two rites for the Mass and we were expected to know them even though we were to be witnesses and assistants at only one, the Roman rite, by far the world and Olympic champion in Western civilization, but there were actually two other Western rites and a startling total of nineteen Eastern Catholic rites, and all twenty-two rites remain in my mind not unlike a poem, and so I chant the Poem of the Twenty-Two Rites, which I dedicate to Father Dennis Whelan, wherever he may be: Abyssinian, Albanian, Ambrosian, Armenian, Bulgarian, Chaldean, Coptic, Georgian, Greek, Hungarian, Italo-Albanian, Malabar, Malankar, Maronite, Melkite, Mozarabic, Roman, Rumanian, Russian, Ruthenian, Serbian, and Syrian. I even remember that the Ambrosian rite was used only in Milan, and the Mozarabic rite only in Toledo and Salamanca in Spain. And then there are the thirteen Masses within the Roman rite: the Missa Cantata, or Sung Mass (or High Mass), sung by a priest and a choir, the Gregorian Masses (a series celebrated for thirty consecutive days for the release of a soul in purgatory), the Low (the "usual Mass," like the ones I assisted Father Whelan with), the Pontifical (said by a bishop), the Solemn (sung by a priest with acolytes, choir, deacon, and subdeacon), the Votive (priest's choice of intentions), Missa Pro Populo (said by pastors by church law eighty-eight times a year), Mass of a Saint, Mass of Exposition, Mass of Reposition, Mass of the Catechumens (the first half of

Mass, before the big moment), Mass of the Faithful (second half), and Mass of the Presanctified (part of the Good Friday Mass during the passion of Christ).

To remember all this, is that prayer or foolishness?

Mass of the Faithful
Once Father Whelan was on his mark, facing the congregation from behind the altar, Mass was underway. The pieces of it snicked into place like oiled parts of an engine. Opening prayers, prayer for the intention of the day, Gospel, Eucharist, serving of the Eucharist along the rail, left to right and back again, cleanup and closing prayers, back to the front of the altar for the brisk procession back into the sacristy. Or, in the order of the Latin prayers we learned and then unlearned, *aufer a nobis, oramus te, Kyrie* (Greek, left over from the first and second centuries A.D. before the Mass went Latin), *Gloria, Alleluia, Credo, Dominus Vobiscum, Oremus, Sanctus, Te igitur, Communicantes, Hanc igitur, Quam oblationem, unde et memores, Supra quae, Supplices, per quem, per ipsum, Pater Noster, Libera nos, Agnus Dei, Domine, Ite missa es, placeat,* and then a rush for the door, or, in the case of the priest and the altar boy, a dignified retreat to the sacristy.

As Whelan ducked back under the sacristy lintel he was a different man, and even before he was across the room you could see the steel go out of his body. At the counter he took off his alb and hung up his cincture on the inside of his closet door. Then he peeled his chasuble off over his head like a boy yanking off a sweater, and then he sat down on his stool and lit a cigar. By then my surplice and cassock were hanging in my locker and I was sitting in one of the two chairs by the door. It was considered bad form to leave the sacristy before Father left. Some boys waited impatiently by the door but I rather liked Whelan and enjoyed the postmortem:

Good job out there, son.

Thank you, Father.

Could do the bells a little sharper.

Yes, Father.

Then still them with your off hand.

Yes, Father.

Are we on next week?

Monday for me, Father.

Ah, that'll be Father Driscoll.

Driscoll was another brisk guy, although not quite so smooth as Whelan. He was a good deal younger and he lingered over the prayers a little. It was said that he had a hair shirt and the stigmata, and we watched his hands closely when he carved the prayers during Mass. You couldn't really tell about the stigmata; there were marks there, but he could have cut himself working in the priests' garden, which was the domain of a little Italian Jesuit who made pickles and such. Driscoll's small hands were always moist, and he had the unusual habit of shaking hands with his altar boys after a Mass; he did this as part of his disrobing ritual, and he would actually come into our little locker room to shake hands if we'd forgotten about it. He always seemed out of place there, and he didn't stay any longer than the handshake.

Once a visiting Franciscan who didn't know the custom wandered into our locker room after a Sunday Mass and sat down companionably. There were four of us boys there at the time, two just finished and two suiting up, and I remember the uncomfortable silences after the priest's friendly questions; we weren't used to a priest in our room, and he was an oddity anyway, with his hooded brown robe and bare feet in enormous sandals. He had gnarled feet like the roots of oak trees. The veins on his feet looked like cables and his toenails were as big as quarters. He finally realized the score and left, after shaking our hands. His hands were a lot bigger and dryer than Father Driscoll's. He didn't have the stigmata.

Years later I realized with a start that Christ probably looked a good deal like the Franciscan, with his dusty feet and pocked face, and I had ignored the guy, wished him gone no less than shaky Peter had wished Jesus gone from his past before the cock crew; Peter standing there in the icy darkness, the fire at his feet sparking up into the dangerous night, sharp voices coming at him like needles, he shifts uneasily from foot to foot and damns his friend as easily, as thoughtlessly, as you might crush a beetle; then a shooting pain of light in the sky, dawn crawls over the hills, and right in his ear, as loud and shrill as a scream, comes the shriek of a rooster and the horrible knowledge that *he has betrayed the man he loves* . . .

Consecration
Actual belief in the miracle was mixed among us boys, although all of us watched the priest's hands with awe at the instant the Host was changed into the living, breathing body of Christ. We did not expect to actually see change steal over the Host itself, as we had been told ad infinitum by the nuns that the miracle was beyond human ken, but we did half expect to see a priest's hands burst spontaneously into flame as he handled the distilled essence of the Mind that invented the universe. There was some discussion about what we should do if a hand fire broke out. There were two general camps: the first insisted that the water cruet should be flung at the fire, and the second advised a sprint away from the awful miracle and toward the janitor, who spoke only shards of English but who knew how to deal with fires, locked doors, broken bicycle chains, vomit, heart attacks, dog bites, broken teeth, broken noses, blood, and sobbing first graders who peed their pants because they were too shy to raise their hands and ask Sister if they could go to the bathroom.

I could never turn my eyes away from that key moment, though. It was and is the single most mysterious and bizarre belief of my faith, and it was in many ways the thing that set us apart from all other Christian denominations. In later years I would sit in Congregationalist and Episcopalian and Lutheran services and observe the communions of those faiths, the passing of torn bread among the faithful and the circulating of cups of wine, and while these acts seemed friendlier to me, more communal than the shivering magic of the transubstantiation, they seemed insubstantial too, muted, more like a casual brunch than a heartbreaking Last Supper. I always wanted to like the communions of other faiths, but they seemed pale to me. I suppose being dipped in miracles every day inoculates you against the mundane—or at least it shoots your sense of perspective all to hell. I still expect miracles, and I have seen some: my wife, my daughter coming out of my wife, my twin sons coming out of my wife one after the other like a circus act, the bolt of light that shot around the room when my uncle died.

Requiem

Recently I went to Mass in the Cathedral of the Madeleine in Salt Lake City. This edifice, a monument to the staying power of Catholicism in the heart of Mormon country, is the church where my late father-in-law was an altar boy in the 1920s. He was also a student there, as the cathedral once housed a grade school in its nether regions (four Congregation of Holy Cross nuns taught eight grades), but it was the altar itself that I was interested in, and during Mass I deliberately detoured past the immense stone altar and proscenium, thinking of the man who once knelt there, garbed in acolyte's robes, draped in youth, not yet the affable patriarch who would sire six children and build a business and hammer a home out of the Oregon woods and die there suddenly among his pastures and gardens, his breath sliding to a halt as his lungs filled with fluid, his wife holding him in her arms as he slumped helplessly to one side of the bed, the look on his face more confusion than pain, his death a great surprise to him on a lovely April morning, the scents of horses and blackberry trickling in the window.

I don't know what I expected to see there, amid the pomp and circumstance of Mass in this garish old castle. I suppose I was looking for the marks of his knees, or the hovering nugget of his soul.

He died before I met him, before I could thank him for his daughter and show him my daughter and sons. I have looked for him in the woods and in the wood of the house he made. I have been closest to him near a small pond that he labored to clear from the woods, but the forest in Oregon is a tenacious thing and it took the pond back after the man died. It is a mouth filled with water. Weeds have grown over it so that it can no longer talk.

Adolesensuous
Certainly being an altar boy was training for the priesthood, in the way that baseball's little leagues are training grounds for the big leagues. We were encouraged to go on outings with the younger priests, who took us to carnivals and baseball games (always the Mets, never the Yankees) and bowling alleys. The eighth graders made a pilgrimage to the seminary at Garrison, New York, every year; the year I went the school had just opened a vast and gleaming sports center, and a quiver of athletic lust went through me like winter wind when the doors to this Xanadu swung open and revealed an oceanic swimming pool and a glittering gymnasium with polished hardwood floors and *glass backboards*. We nearly fainted with desire. The young priest showing off this gem had the wit to remain silent as we gaped at Neverland, and my friends and I spent the rest of the day envisioning ourselves sprinting and spinning and scoring thousands of points on that perfect floor, the stands throbbing with local girls tantalized not only by our patent skill but by the thought that we were tadpole priests—how much more enticing to lure a prospective saint down into the willow trees by the river, and there slip a tongue in his mouth and get his hand on your breast and see if the Catholic Church in the vaguely sanctified person of this gangly zit of a boy was indeed convinced that asceticism was a road to holiness.

Combine this athletic Xanadu with the sweeping view of the Hudson Valley below, and the lush playing fields terracing off into the distance, and the sense that a boy living at a high school fully two hours from home was an independent and mature creature, and you had a potent draw for boys on the lip of puberty; but then we were served mystery meat for lunch, in a dank military-style cafeteria, and shown through the cold moist barracks, where narrow metal cots stretched away for miles, where a thousand boys had pulled the pud in a thousand slate-gray stalls, and they lost us. All the way home Father Driscoll chirped the virtues of the seminary but we were silent, each boy afraid to be the first to burst the poor man's bubble. He might, after all, bear the stigmata; plus we felt sorry for him. He had once been sentenced to a narrow cot and horse burgers and dismal mornings pulling his pud in a dank gray stall where cockroaches did the fandango through scummy puddles.

We went home to our bright houses with joy.

Catechumens
On mornings when I had the 6:00 Mass I awoke in the woolly dark and left my brothers snoring like bears and pedaled through the empty streets with my fists clenched in my jacket pockets and my collar turned up against the whip of dawn. The church was silent and dark. The only light in it was the tabernacle lamp, and the only sign of human life the stray Styrofoam coffee cups filled with cigarette butts in the back of the church, the spoor of the Nocturnal Adoration Society, which met once a month to conduct a vigil with the Blessed Sacrament, which reposed inside a monstrance on the altar; teams of men would arrive every hour and replace the team in the church, each team yawning as it passed the other, exchanging muted greetings, a handshake here and there in the dark air, the men checking their watches and settling down on their knees like old horses waiting for dawn.

There were seven lay societies: the Altar Society (for women), the Blessed Virgin Sodality (for young women), the Holy Name Society (for men), the Legion of Mary, the Mother's Club, the Nocturnal Adoration Society (for men), and the Rosary Society (for women). While my ambition was to someday join my father in the Nocturnal Adoration Society, my admiration was highest for the Altar Society, whose members worked liked bees to keep the church and its accouterments sparkling. "It was they who undertook the laundering of altar linens, communion cloths and surplices, the polishing of the brass candelabra and altar vases, as well as the disposal of withered flowers, ferns, and pot plants," as the Irish writer Mary Lavin recounts in her story "A Voice from the Dead." They were an efficient lot, friendly but brisk, and the Good Lord Himself could not help a boy who got in their way when they were stripping the altar linens; more than once I was shouldered against the cold wall of the sacristy by a brisk Altar Society woman with an armful of God's laundry, on her way purposefully, moving through the waters of the day like a battleship, to her dank basement laundry room and the magic Maytag thundering away like the monstrous engine of a ship.

Incense
Almost always I was at the church before Father Whelan. I would hear his steps in the courtyard and smell his cigar. He smoked villainous cigars, execrable things that smelled like peat moss and burned fitfully if at all. He was always at them, lighting, relighting, puffing determinedly, moaning with despair at the shoddy plug that hung like a zeppelin between his lips. He got them from the tobacconist in the village, a seedy man with a harelip who gave the priests a break, 20 percent off, probably in exchange for future considerations. I know the price because I once bought a box for Whelan after Mass; he'd been caught short, and after thrashing his pockets like a man with bees on his pecker, he sat me down in the sacristy.

I need a favor, son.

Yes, Father.

It's unorthodox.

Yes, Father.

I need cigars.
Cigars?
Cigars. A box of them.
Yes, Father.
You'll have to go up to the village. You have a bike.
Yes, Father.
Get a box of panatelas. Here's a fiver.
Yes, Father.
Don't smoke any.
No, Father.
Keep the change.
Yes, Father.
None of these coronas, now.
Yes, Father.
What?
I mean No, Father.

Memento
I remember the dark scent of the church at dawn, the dense purple light, the smells of incense and cigars and dust. I remember the dry shuffling of shoes as communicants shambled toward the Host. I remember the twisted faces of saints in the windows, Veronica's pale hand outstretched with a cloth for the face of Christ, the bulging Popeye forearm of Simon as he supported the collapsing Savior. I remember the groaning organ and the reverberating yowl of an infant being baptized in the nave. I remember the stiff black cloth under which you hid all desire and personality as you prepared to assist at a miracle that you did not and could never understand but that you watched for ravenously, like a hawk after meat. For a time we were expected to wear ties under our cassocks but eventually this stricture was lifted and we were allowed to wear shirts. No jeans, no sneakers, no sandals—this last despite the gnarled treelike feet of the Franciscans on the altar once a month. You buttoned your cassock from the bottom up, to be sure of

symmetry, and then you slipped on the starched white surplice. A simple uniform, black and white, unornamented, memorable.

Credo
I have come, in my middle years, to a passionate belief in a Coherence—a pervasive divineness that I only dimly comprehend and cannot at all articulate. It is a feeling, a sense. I feel it most near my elfin daughter, my newborn sons. Last night I stood over the huddled body of my daughter, asleep in her crib, her hair flowing around her like dark water. She had sobbed herself to sleep only minutes before, after soiling herself and her bedding and her bear. She is very sick and cannot control her bowels and she is humiliated and frightened by this; she fell asleep in my wife's arms, her sobs muffled in the folds of my wife's deep soft flannel shirt. I stand above her now in the dark. She is curled like a question in the corner of her crib. I place my hands together in an ancient gesture of prayer and humility and begin to weep—for love of this child, in fear of illness, in despair at my helplessness. I make a prayer in the dark. I believe so strongly, so viscerally, in a wisdom and vast joy under the tangled weave of the world, under the tattered blanket of our evil and tragedy and illness and brokenness and sadness and loss, that I cannot speak it, cannot articulate it, but can only hold on to ritual and religion like a drowning man to a sturdy ship.

Benedicamus Domino
"And so the Mass comes to an end, in a whirl of purifications and postscripts that do not seek to impress themselves deeply on the mind; one has not enough capacity left for receiving impressions," wrote the English priest and novelist Ronald Knox. "'And every man went to his own house,' as it says frequently in the Old Testament and once in the New, and that is what we do; we must be alone."

Many a time I was alone, when it was all over, when the rail-birds had gone from the rail, when the businessmen were walking briskly to their trains. When the audience was gone the janitor would whip through the church slamming the kneelers back up and slipping missals and songbooks back into their racks behind each pew. Then he would bow before the altar and slip out a side door toward the school. I would wait for the click of the side door closing and then wander out of the sacristy and sit down in a pew and think and listen and wait for something to happen. The building groaned and creaked, the candles fluttered and sizzled, bees and flies bounced off the windows. In the windows were the saints, red and blue and green and pink, their faces and bodies and fluttering hands outlined in lead. After a few minutes I would walk down the aisle, past the empty pews and kneelers and missals and stations of the cross, and push through the massive oak door and into the broad fat light of the new day, dazzled.

Father, Son,
Spirit Holy

D inner hour, and I sit down to table with my wife and three
small children, ready to talk turkey. Today it is my youngest
son's turn for grace, and he starts us off with the sign of the cross.
He has a unique take on this act, as in so many other aspects of his
life: not unlike a third-base coach, he makes a flurry of motions,
touching forehead, belly, shoulders, nose, temples, ears, and
(finally) tongue, all the while chanting, at a terrific pace, "Father,
Son, Spirit Holy."

As usual, he sends his family into stitches, and after a while we
bring him around to a slightly more orthodox sign of the cross, but
as his mother and sister and brother recover from the giggles and
set to work editing their meals, his father's mind, as usual, rambles.
Whence came this unusual motion of the hand and incantation?
Why do we mark moments great and small, holy and horrendous,
with this gentle handmade echo of the crucifix? *Father, Son, Holy
Ghost*, I whispered as a boy, and *Father, Son, Holy Spirit*, I whisper
as a man, in moments of joy and fear, prayer and penitence. I make

the sign of the cross in wonder when my children do or say something that slaps me into remembering that they came to me from the hand of the Lord. I make the sign in gratitude when they finally fall asleep. I make it in desperate prayer when they are wan and weak and sick. I make it before meals, during Masses, after funerals, after baptisms; I make it in awe and epiphany and tragedy.

I do it all the time, and I am by no means alone; no other simple physical gesture is so widespread among Catholics. More than sinking to our knees, more than folding our hands together in prayer, more than bowing our heads under blessings, it is the making of the sign of the cross with our hands that marks us as Catholics—as men and women (and small children) who believe in the risen Christ, the God and man who died on a wooden crucifix on the Hill of Skulls, long centuries ago.

Scholars trace the practice back as far as the year A.D. 110, by which time it was already established as a common gesture among Christians—most common, apparently, among those Christian communities associated with St. Paul. "Its format is a simple geometry," said the late Congregation of Holy Cross theologian Rev. Jeffrey Sobosan. "It traces out a cross in the sequence of four points touched: head to chest, shoulder to shoulder. The early Christians thought it was the way Jesus *died*, far more than the way He *lived* prior to His arrest, that constituted the saving act whereby He pleased God." So those early Christian cults honored, in a simple physical gesture, the geometric shape on which Christ gave his life for us.

It is a small miracle, perhaps, that this gesture has persisted unchanged throughout many nations and centuries—but miracles are not unusual, are they?

Such a simple act, our hands cutting the air like the wings of birds, fingers alighting gently on our bodies in memory of the body broken for us:

"Father," we say, touching our heads, the seats of our cerebrations, and we think of the Maker, that vast incomprehensible Coherence stitching everything together, and

"Son," touching our hearts, and feeling the ache and exhaustion of the Father's Son, the God-made-man, the gaunt dusty tireless fellow who walked and talked endlessly through the hills of Judea, who knew what would happen to him, who accepted it with amazing grace, who died screaming so that we might live past death, and

"Holy," touching the left shoulder, on which we carry hope, and

"Spirit," touching the right shoulder, on which we carry love,

and the gesture is done, hanging in the air like a memory, its line traced on our bodies as if printed there by the thousands of times our hands have marked it. I make it in the dark, over my sleeping children; I make it at dawn, staring at the incredible world waking; I make it smiling, cheered by the persistence of miracles; I make it sobbing over the corpse of a friend in a wooden coffin, returned now to the Carpenter who made him.

Simple, powerful, poignant, the sign of the cross is a mnemonic device like the Mass, in which we sit down to table with one another and remember the Last Supper, or like a baptism, where we remember John the Baptist's brawny arm pouring some of the Jordan River over Christ. So we remember the central miracle and paradox of the faith that binds us each to each: that we believe, against all evidence and sense, in life and love and light, in the victory of those things over death and evil and darkness.

Such a ferocious and brave notion, to be hinted at by such a simple motion, and the gesture itself lasting perhaps all of four seconds, if you touch all the bases and don't rush. But simple as the sign of the cross is, it carries a brave weight: it names the Trinity, celebrates the Creator, and brings home all the power of faith to the brush of fingers on skin and bone and belly. So do we, sometimes well and sometimes ill, labor to bring home our belief in God's love to the stuff of our daily lives, the skin and bone of this world—and the sign of the cross helps us to remember that we have a Companion on the road.

The Mass Is a Genius

A nd I'll tell you why.

Because each and every Mass celebrated over the course of many centuries in many lands under every conceivable condition in every conceivable surrounding and language has gathered a random aggregate of people together for a miracle meal in the name of the Christ, and the whole point of Christ and the church that grew up in his name is to gather random aggregates of people in communion with the divine.

So the Mass is a constant and consistent microcosm of meaning.

Because while the Mass is a repetitive ritual, each one is different from every other one, in tone, volume, length, character, flavor, light, and population—not unlike the way human beings, while all human, are utterly different each from each.

So the Mass is just like the creatures who come to it for sustenance and succor.

Because the miracle at the very heart of the Mass, the mysterious conversion of bread into the veritable body of Christ, is wholly inexplicable and, let's be completely honest here, unbelievable— just like the miracle at the very heart of Catholicism itself, which is summed up tersely by the enormous phrase "Christ has died, Christ has risen, Christ will come again." But we *do* believe these things, against all sense and evidence, against the great weight of the opinion of the world.

So the Mass contains within it a miracle exactly as mysterious and confusing and confounding as the more momentous miracle that causes the Mass itself to occur, day after day after day.

Because the Mass has a central figure around whom the action revolves, the celebrant, but is designed and performed for all present, the congregation. Or, in other words, the play is performed by a troupe, one of whom is the prime actor with the best lines, but the hero of the play arrives in the middle of the performance, after which he is present but unseen, and what the troupe performs, or reenacts, or remembers, or celebrates, is in part the hero's demise and startling return, which is echoed in the Eucharist, when what was dross is suddenly divine.

Because the Mass is endlessly capable of reinvention and recalibration, has proven itself wonderfully amenable to taking what is given (the local political scene, the language, the physical circumstances of room, wet hedgerow, icy foxhole, steaming hold of fetid ship) and making of them moments of immense power and grace.

Because the Mass, like all geniuses, may just as easily break down and be reduced without warning to a shell of itself, an echo of what it was or might have been, an amazement gone awry, a delight dulled.

In short the Mass is a genius because like genius it is a mystery that we find enticing and necessary; because it cuts jagged bright holes in the unknown and shoves us closer to what we might call wisdom, or God; because it appears to be a wholly normal and orthodox vehicle in which is found, inexplicably, the stunning.

What is the Mass? It is the shuffling of everyman to a meal and familiar table talk; but somehow at the picnic table, the dining-room table, the rickety card table where the children sit, there is, as the basket of bread is passed from hand to hand, a flicker of light, a brief zest in the air like the spoor of lightning, a voice singing powerfully in the distance, a few blocks away, past the neighbors' neighbors' houses, and you strain to hear it, and it's the most extraordinary snatch of song you ever heard—and the Mass is over, go in peace, and you do.

A Sunday, in October, under a Flight of Geese

A little Catholic university chapel, all cedar and sunlight, amid a riot of rhododendrons.

Behind the chapel, a crowd of muscular old oak trees.

Before it, a sea of fresh-cut grass dotted with scrawny cherry trees, toddlers, dandelions.

Above it, a ragged arrowhead of geese, southing.

Sounds: pants legs scissoring toward Mass, small talk by the front door, chirping children, a metronomic phoebe, an organ playing Bach's Fugue in C Minor.

Inside: a small child with his right arm in the baptismal font up to his shoulder. Child's father turns and notices son's oar in the water, emits indescribable sound, carts boy off to dry pew.

Mass begins, gently.

There are perhaps 150 people here this morning, the great majority of them undergraduates, although it's an all-ages show, and from the balcony where I ride herd on my three small children I see gray hair, white hair, green hair, blue hair, no hair.

My children, interested and hungry, eat crackers.

"This morning we gather as a faith community to broaden our vision," says the young priest. He will utter the word *community* seven times this morning, by my count, and tribal binding is the clear theme of this Mass. Two other priests are robed and on the altar, and the whole crowd sings lustily, holds hands while chanting the Our Father, exchanges hearty handshakes of peace at startling length (one energetic boy making his way completely around the chapel). All but a handful will receive communion; all but a handful will stay after Mass to chat in cheerful knots; all, apparently, are excited and stimulated by Mass. This crowd isn't dutiful; it's pumped. Rumors of death of faith among youth are greatly exaggerated, at least this morning.

The Gospel, from Mark, is about the apostles James and John, who itch for good seats in heaven and demand same of the Rabbi. Christ fires back classic Christly conundrum: he who wishes to be great must be a servant.

Homily: "Not the most flattering portrait of James and John, is it? They ask for prestige and power, and Christ rebukes them sharply, as he rebukes us, all these years later, as we itch for power too. Be honest: Don't you wish for status among your peers? Don't you want to be first and best? We're more like James and John than we like to admit, and as usual Christ disturbs us . . ."

My children, having marched through crackers and gingersnaps, are now eating grapes.

Eucharist: at the moment of transformation the priest pauses for a tremulous instant, and the whole chapel is riveted and silent as he hoists *I am who am* aloft—and then comes the communion shuffle, the sharp smell of mediocre wine, dry crackers on tongues, another hymn, the bowed meditating heads, blessing and dismissal, *another* hymn, and then the organ groans awake and sends us out again into the light, where the phoebe is still keeping time, and for no reason, every reason, I am delighted, my pockets filled with grapes, my pinkies gripped by small boys, my morning mad with miracles.

part four

Revelations & Epiphanies

*I believe that the fingerprints of
the Maker are everywhere:
children, hawks, water . . .*

Eating Dirt

I have a small daughter and two smaller sons, twins. They are all three in our miniscule garden at the moment, my sons eating dirt as fast as they can get it off the planet and down their gullets. They are two years old, they were seized with dirt-fever an instant ago, and as admirably direct and forceful young men, quick to act, true sons of the West, they are going to *eat some dirt*, boy, and you'd better step aside.

My daughter and I step aside.

The boys are eating so much dirt so fast that much of it is missing their maws and sliding muddily down their chicken chests. It is thick moist dirt, slightly more solid than liquid. I watch a handful as it travels toward the sun. It's rich brown stuff, almost black, crumbly. In it there are a couple of tiny pebbles, the thin lacy bones of a former leaf (alder? hawthorn?), the end of a worm, the tiny green elbows of bean sprouts. In a moment I will pull the boys over and issue a ticket and a stern speech about eating beans before their time, but right now I watch with interest as one boy

91

inserts the dirt, chews meditatively, emits a wriggling worm, stares at it—and eats it again.

"Dad, they're *eating the garden*," says my daughter.

So they are. I'll stop them soon, before they eat more of the world than they should, but for this rare minute in life we are all absorbed by dirt, our faces to the ground, and I feel, inarticulately, that there's something simple and true going on here, some lesson they should absorb, so I let them absorb dirt.

It occurs to me that we all eat dirt. Fruits and vegetables are dirt transformed by light and water. Animals are vigorous dirt, having dined on fruit or vegetables or other animals who dine on flora. Our houses and schools and offices are cupped by dirt and made of wood and stone and brick—former dirt. Glass is largely melted sand, a kind of clean dirt. Our clothing used to be dirt. Paper was trees was dirt. We shape dirt into pots, plates, mugs, vases. We breathe dirt suspended in the air, we crunch it between our teeth on spinach leaves and fresh carrots, we wear it in the lines of our hands and the folds of our faces, we catch it in the linings of our noses and eyes and ears. Some people are driven by private fires to eat dirt, often during pregnancy—the condition is called pica, from the Latin word for magpie.

In short we swim in an ocean of dirt, yet we hardly ever consider it closely, except to plumb it for its treasures, or furrow it for seed, or banish it from our persons, clothes, houses. We're suckers for *dramatic* former dirt—cougars, lilies, bears, redwoods—but don't often reflect on the basic stuff itself: good old simple regular normal orthodox there-it-sits-under-everything dirt.

My sons, filled with fill, turn their attentions to the other denizens of the garden: bamboo, beetles, blackberries, carrots, camellias, cedars, dandelions, dockweed, garlic, hawthorn, jays, moles, shrews, slugs, snails, spiders, squirrels—all made of dirt, directly or indirectly.

I am hardly handy about the house and garden, and I spend my hours on other matters, but enough of me feels responsible for the dirt that surrounds my home that I have often regretted the general reckless abandonment of my garden, and felt a certain guilt that it is not productive, that the land lies fallow, that little food for our table grows there. But now, sitting against the old fence, cradling my daughter, grinning at the mud monkeys, I see that the garden is *itself* hard at work, hatching honey ants and potato bugs, propelling bamboo and beans into the air, serving as a grocery store for shrews. I imagine it in one of those time-lapse film clips, madly roiling with animals and plants, the sun and rain baking and hammering it at a terrific pace, the banks of clouds sliding over like vast battleships.

Such busy dirt.

The children tire, the sun retreats, in we go to baths and beds. I wash the garden off my sons. It swirls down the bathtub drain, into the river, eventually to the ocean. So some of my garden ends up as silt, some sinks to the ocean floor, some becomes kelp and razor clams and sea otters, some is drawn up again into rain—and maybe some returns to the garden, after a nearly unimaginable vacation.

My daughter and I discuss the journeys of dirt.

And when the rain begins that evening, the first of the rains that define fall and winter here, she and I draw a map for our dirt, so that it will know how to come home to our house, and we leave the map on the back porch for the dirt to read.

"Maybe there are dirt fairies," says my daughter. "Or maybe the dirt can read. Who knows?"

Maybe my daughter—named for a flower that flows up from the dirt with extraordinary thin-necked elegance and lift—is right about this. Maybe the dirt *can* read. Certainly, in a very real sense, the dirt can write: consider, for example, this essay, made by dirt worked in wondrous ways into bone, blood, protein, water, and electricity.

So dirt leans against a fence with lovely dirt in his lap, and watches dirt demons devour dirt, and the world spins in its miraculous mysterious circles, dust unto dust.

Such busy dirt, such a blizzard of blessings.

The Anchoviad

My daughter, age six, sleeps with her bear, also age six. My son, age three, sleeps with his basketball and a stuffed tiger, age unknown. My other son, also age three, sleeps with a can of anchovy fillets—King Oscar brand, caught off the coast of Morocco and distributed by the H. J. Nosaki Company in New York.

He sleeps with the can every night, won't go to sleep without it under his right cheek. The can is bright red and features a drawing of King Oscar, an avuncular, bearded fellow, apparently a benevolent despot. Every night after Liam is asleep I gently delete the can from his grip and examine it. It's a roll-key can, fifty-six grams, with "about six fillets (15g)." Other than the friendly visage of King Oscar, my favorite thing about the can is the word *about*, a rare concession, in the corporate world, to ambiguity. I suppose it's a legal thing, but still it pleases me, for murky reasons.

I sit there in the dark, holding the anchovies, and ponder other murky things like: What's the deal with this boy and his anchovies?

How is it that we are drawn to the odd things we love? How came anchovies from Morocco to be swimming headless under my son's cheek in Oregon? What do we know about anchovies other than their savory saltiness? What do we really know well about *any* creature, including and most of all ourselves, and how is it that even though we know painfully little about anything, we often manage world-wrenching hubris about our wisdom?

Consider the six animals in the can. They are members of the family Engraulidae, the anchovies, which range in size from a Brazilian anchovy the size of your thumbnail to a ravenous New Guinea anchovy as long as your forearm. Anchovies don't survive in captivity, and they don't survive long after being netted either, so we know little about them—but that little is riveting:

- Their hearing is perhaps the sharpest of any marine animal's, and the frequency they hear best is, eerily, exactly the frequency of the tail beats of other fish. Is it their unimaginably crisp hearing that allows them to swim in darting collectives that twist as one astonishing creature? We don't know.
- Their noses contain a sensory organ that no other creature in the world has. What's it for? No one knows.
- Sensory complexes are present in anchovies' heads, and they also form dense nets in their cheeks. What do these nets do? A puzzle.
- Anchovies get their food by dragging their open mouths through the ocean in mammoth schools, but what, exactly, do they eat? Surprise: no one knows.

Among the species of anchovy are, to the delight of meditative fathers sitting in the dark on their sons' beds, the buccaneer anchovy (which ranges furthest into the open ocean), and the sabretooth anchovy, which has very large teeth and hangs around, understandably, by itself. And I do not even mention the anchovies' cousin, the wolf herring, which grows to be a yard long, and has so many teeth that it has teeth on its *tongue*.

Thus the anchovy: fully as mysterious a creature as, well, this boy sleeping with the fishes. And what, really, do I know irrefutably about my son? Some of his quirks, a bit of his character, his peculiar dietary habits, the lilt of his song, the ache of his sob, where his scars are, the way his hair wants to go, the knock of his knees—and not much else. He is a startling, one-time-only, boneheaded miracle with a sensory complex in his head and heart that I can only guess at and dimly try to savor in the few brilliant moments I have been given to swim with him. He is a sort of anchovy, as are we all; so I sing our collective salty song—the song of fast, mysterious, open-mouthed creatures, traveling with vast schools of our fellows, listening intently, savoring the least of our brethren, and doing our absolute level best to avoid the wolf herring.

Diary: Summer

Tuesday

Woke up to find a mosquito the size of a dog sitting on my chest. Knocked her to the floor with a pillow and stuffed her out the window before she quite regained her wits.

Wednesday

Spent an hour talking to a fisherman. He was fishing for perch but wanted to talk about the halibut not far offshore. "There's halibut out there as big as doors," he said. We both stared out to sea silently and respectfully for a moment.

Thursday

Two sea lions, a male and female, hauled themselves up on the beach this morning. The male looked like a dissolute Trent Lott and spent his day snarling at dogs. The dogs kept running up to the lions with the usual cocky canine curiosity and then, when

Lott reared and roared, slamming into reverse so fast that once one did a somersault.

Friday
My young twin sons and I experimented with botanical acoustics: which leaves make the coolest sound when you pee on them? Winner: skunk cabbage.

Saturday
Counted dead creatures along the beach: murres, gulls, crabs, sea lettuce, kelp, clams, mussels, most of a young seal, and something that had been reduced to a shiny pelvis. Lost count after two minutes. Pondered life, death, cycle of it all, and whose pelvis that used to be.

Sunday
Discovered that the sea rocket, the plant that grows furthest out into the sand from the protective mother ship of the dunes, responds to burial in sand with enhanced growth and more seeds per plant. The sheer roaring energy of things is stunning, miraculous, holy, a prayer, inexplicable, I give up. There is no word eloquent enough for the vast passion of living things.

Monday
A neighbor told me the story of an 1886 wreck on this shore, of a Welsh ship called the *Carmarthan Castle*, carrying wheat, wood, and a rooster. Captain and crew survived wreck; rooster lost at sea. Rooster had been around Cape Horn three times. That was one tough rooster. Wonder who ate him? All creatures are essentially tough, it seems to me, even the most fragile ones. Maybe the fragile ones are the toughest of all.

Tuesday
Watched robins at work for a while. They cocked their heads and listened carefully and then stabbed into the grass and yanked out a meal. *They heard worms moving.*

Wednesday
Fistfight broke out this afternoon between small twin sons. Draw. Interesting mammals, sons—quick, muscled, aggressive, loud, small, cunning, appealing. The whole essence of human maturity, I suppose, is to turn natural mammalian aggression into focused passion. Meanwhile, both boys sent to dungeon.

Thursday
Brooding weather all day, then a furious downpour, then *brilliant* late afternoon sun, the air crisp and clean and everything dripping happily, all creatures emerged blinking and capering, the sky crammed with wheeling swifts, you could see for miles, the air so freshly washed that your lungs grinned. You know what I mean.

Friday
Watched adult starling trudge around with wailing progeny trailing so close behind that it stumbled on the heels of its parent. Parent must have been a father; it turned around occasionally and glared at its whining child so ferociously that I quailed.

Saturday
My daughter made a remark so piercing, so poignant, so penetrating, so startlingly reflective for a human being of any age that I gaped. The whole point of higher intelligence and complex language is to connect to other beings in ways that produce moments of epiphany like this, no? And perhaps those moments advance our moral evolution, which perhaps saves the world we share. Perhaps.

Sunday
Sitting in church, I noted all the former trees at work: beams of fir, roof of hemlock and pine, floor of white oak, walls and altar and chairs and kneelers and lectern of cherry, doors of walnut.

Monday
Friend of mine died last night, at age forty-five, of Lou Gehrig's disease. He was a terrific athlete and a witty man. All that grace and humor melting back into the earth, gone but not gone; his grin hangs in the air like a Cheshire cat's.

Tuesday
Friend from abroad ate his first blackberry in America. "Tastes like another language," he said, startled.

Reading the Birds

Big birds: a golden eagle, huge and huddled, its head drawn down between its shoulders against hissing snow, standing forlornly on a pine branch like a sorrowful monk. Two young bald eagles, not yet hooded with white, launching together from a Sitka spruce like two immense prayers; the bough they gripped shivers for a moment, remembering. A red-tailed hawk the size of a toddler sliding from an oak snag onto a rabbit; the rabbit screams twice, a thin awful whistle; the hawk drapes its wings over the scene like a curtain. Last, largest, a baleful condor in a zoo cage, staring at awed children, its unblinking hooded yellow eyes forgetting nothing.

Small birds: a hummingbird the color of joy. A wren in a winter thicket, a circle amid lines. A sparrow, tiny and cocky, shouting at cars and dogs. A finch pouring summer from its mouth. A tree swallow, no bigger than the hand of a child, carving the huge air into circles of iridescent green and blue and black. It swims and

slices through the air. It is as light as a whip tip. It is made of sunlight and insect juice, exuberance and desire.

*

Once, years ago, I had my own woods. My wife and I were care-
takers of the house that anchored them, that rose above them like
a shambling wooden castle. The house and its woods stood on a
muscle of earth called Snake Hill.

I spent a great deal of time in the woods of Snake Hill, collecting kindling, tracking pheasants in snow, reading the runes
of twigs. Many twilights I stood and watched buttery last light
spatter through oaks, birches, beeches. One evening I noticed
five immense birds in a maple. They were huddled together like
a feathered fist. They were each nearly three feet tall, they
hunched their heads like shy children, they lurched out of the
tree at dusk with the gracelessness of small sofas. But they
were not graceless long; within a second or two they unfurled
their enormous wings and flapped away croaking, groaning,
sobbing. Far below I gaped at their huge silhouettes against the
corduroy sky.

They were night herons. I learned this from a neighbor who
knew his neighbors. We stood under the tree one night and
watched the herons soar away. It was my neighbor's firm opinion
that we should know the names of our neighbors, that residence
entailed self-education, that full life in a place meant knowing the
creatures of that place. He believed that stories were ways to live,
and so he collected and told stories with an eagerness that belied
his age and failing health.

Those five feathered stories meant a great deal to me. Sitting in
that tree, slicing through the woolen twilight, they blessed my
house, my land, my residence on Snake Hill. They added awe and
savor to the woods. They excited the landscape, underlined its

wildness, underscored the fact that it belonged to no one and was only borrowed by the house and people in its midst.

*

Wimbledon, England, some years ago. Eventual lawn tennis champion Stefan Edberg of Sweden winds up for a backhand return to his opponent, Boris Becker of Germany. Suddenly a pied wagtail, a tiny British bird, zooms right across Edberg's line of vision, perhaps a foot from his face. He hits his shot deep into the stands, then scowls, then laughs. The television announcer informs the audience worldwide that a family of pied wagtails has taken up residence in Centre Court's eaves. The British, ever respectful of hearth and home, have not seen it fit to evict the birds.

Starlings take up residence in eaves, dryers, garages, attics, air conditioner vents. The tiny flycatchers called phoebes set up nests on porch lights. So do barn swallows. Swallows and barn owls live in barns, toolsheds, abandoned farmhouses, unattended shacks. Guillemots live on abandoned docks and wharves and wrecks. Peregrine falcons nest on skyscrapers and bridges. Pigeons live under bridges and highway abutments.

I remember the house sparrows that lived for years in our garage when I was a boy; their eggs fell from the roof every spring like slow blue rain.

Once, on a wet Easter morning, I found a fallen sparrow chick on the concrete floor of the garage. It was a male, about a week old. He was twisted, small, deceased. Sometime during the night he had fallen, or had been shoved by his siblings from their disheveled nest in the eaves. My brothers and I buried him in a crayon box. We prayed over the gaudy coffin. My youngest brother sobbed uncontrollably. The broken chick did not rise from the dead, as we hoped but did not expect. My brother says that ever after he looked upon Jesus with a jaundiced eye and wondered at the potency of a story that could not stir life in something so small as a shriveled sparrow.

*

Human beings are attached to the world by intricate strings of memory and desire. We make of our sensory impressions the stuff of a life, a career, a love affair, a story. Birds are players in this drama; they flit about us, encapsulating the ways that we feel, acting as poems, as prayers. I once cried at the sight of a sparrow's defiant, thin-legged stance because it was a speck of unbearable delight in a black time.

Perhaps birds are the most powerful poems for the youngest human beings. The writer Richard Lewis, director of a children's art center in New York City, annually has his young students make bird masks and don them and then tell stories about the birds that they are. "My bird is in you," said Joel, eight years old. "His name is imagination. He lives in a place called heart brain body. It is in everyone. Some adults think it is childish but it will never leave you even if you hide it."

Birds are in us, in our stories of ourselves. Raven stole the sun from heaven and gave it to the Northwest Indian tribes; Raven carried messages from the gods for the Vikings; Raven was the wisest of all creatures in Irish mythology. Eagle gave the Iroquois the dew, made the wind for the Chippewa, tore Prometheus's liver from his body day after day. Wrens and cranes fly through the legends of St. Kevin of Glendalough, swallows and doves through stories of St. Francis, crows through the lore of the Desert Fathers.

They are still in our stories. The day after my father-in-law died, his widow noticed a robin persistently trying to enter their house through what had been her husband's favorite window. The bird tried to get in for a week, always through the same window. I explained to her that the robin, an aggressively territorial bird in season, was probably trying to drive off the intruder he saw reflected in the glass. She listened politely and was not convinced. Ever after there has been a soft place in her heart for robins. For her they are symbols, messages, memories in feathered jackets; for her, robins are bits of her husband, whom she loved desperately and completely, whom she misses most in spring, when robins return and he does not.

*

I have seen many eagles, none low or reduced to this dimension, each lord of the immediate air. They freeze the creatures below them. I have seen a yearling blacktail deer flinch when an eagle's cold shadow passed by. Recently I stood on a high hill in Sitka spruce country, on the Oregon coast, trying to read history by trees: ancient hemlocks in inaccessible ravines, second-growth spruce near trails, alder and brush on open hillsides. Suddenly, silently, two bald eagles were above me. Their shadows swept over the woods, over thickets of salal, salmonberry, blackberry. The hills held their breath. One eagle screamed twice; both eagles slid over the ridgeline and were gone; a wren piped; time resumed.

Walt Whitman saw bald eagles once, over his native Long Island. They were performing their mating dance, a violent swirling waltz conducted wholly in air. Old Walt, characteristically, got the sight down in one enormous sentence. "Skyward in air a sudden muffled sound, the dalliance of the eagles, / " he wrote, "The rushing amorous contact high in space together, / The clinching interlocking claws, a living, fierce, gyrating wheel, / Four beating wings, two beaks, a swirling mass tight grappling, / In tumbling turning clustering loops, straight downward falling, / Till o'er the river pois'd, the twain yet one, a moment's lull, / A motionless still balance in the air, then parting, talons loosing, / Upward again on slow-firm pinions slanting, their separate diverse flight, / She hers, he his, pursuing."

She hers, he his, pursuing.

*

They are creatures from other universes, performing physical feats we can only imagine. A peregrine falcon in full stoop upon a duck is the fastest autonomous creature in the history of the world, reaching a speed of perhaps two hundred miles an hour just before it collides with its prey. It has been designed, over many thousands of years, to be a bullet of feathers and toothpick bones and knife fingers. A golden eagle can see a rabbit's ear twitch from two miles away. A screech owl can hear a mouse running a hundred feet away. An albatross, nine feet wide with wings outstretched, spends nearly its entire life floating over the ocean; it sleeps on the wing, dozing amid billows. The rufous-sided hummingbird, the common tiny hummer of the Pacific Northwest, has a heart rate of some three hundred beats per minute—almost five times as fast as the average human heart rate. ("*Everything* about a hummingbird is a superlative," wrote the naturalist Tom Colazo.)

The implications of its heart rate intrigue me. Does the hummingbird live faster than we do? Does the hummingbird literally live in a different time zone? Time must be made of a different liquid for the hummingbird, since he goes through it so quickly. I imagine my life running five times faster. It seems to run too fast now, and I am a man with a peaceable wife and one small child.

*

The first word my daughter learned, other than the labels she has used since for her parents, was *bird*. I think this is because birds moved across her nascent vision in delightful ways. I spent many hours, in her first few months, holding her against my shoulder so that she could see out a large window. The window overlooks cedar, fir, spruce, laurel, honeysuckle. In the trees and bushes live sparrows, juncos, warblers, jays, starlings, flickers, robins, crows. The trees are green, the bushes are red, the birds are Joseph's coat.

In the chimney of the house next door are brick-brown chimney swifts, which issue forth in a dark cloud at dusk. They swirl and swim in the air like dreams.

Many times I shifted a bit in my chair and felt my daughter's pumpkin head resting against my shoulder and assumed she had fallen asleep, and then turned slightly to see her eyes, and saw them wide open and filled with birds. One day she told me what she saw, muttering wetly in my ear, her feathery voice a pale blue sound, a faint flutey note from a new country. "Bird," she whispered, "Bird, Bird."

Now, a year later, when she sees Bird she does not name him, but blows him a kiss, as she does to family and friends. She holds her fingers over her tiny pursed lips and then swings her hand out and away into the air. Her linked fingers float in the air for a curved instant like a wing.

*

They are travelers beyond our imagination. I once lived along the New England shore, in the middle of what ornithologists call the Atlantic Flyway. Every September hundreds of thousands of birds funneled through the air over my head. Hawks, eagles, falcons, and vultures, while only a fraction of the millions of birds sailing along the coast, were the biggest and most dramatic of the migrants. Ordinarily solitary hunters, they band together in the fall not out of camaraderie but because they all ride rising columns of warm air along ridges and hills. From September through November it's possible to see hundreds, sometimes thousands, of hawks and falcons rising together from the woods, a reverse rain of raptors, all intent on gaining soaring height for their trips to Central and South America.

For the raptors this little autumnal jaunt can mean two thousand miles in the air. The arctic tern sneers at that trip; it travels from one pole to the other in its migration. Other birds travel short distances thoroughly. Hummingbirds have rectangular territories a few yards wide. Wrens have slightly larger territories, perhaps a hundred yards square. Western jays have territories with ceilings: at sea level is the scrub jay; in the woods is the Steller's jay; at high elevations is the whiskey jack, or camp robber; and at the tree line is Clark's nutcracker, the jay closest to heaven. (The bird is named for Captain William Clark, the first white man to describe it; Clark himself was led to the Northwest by a Shoshone woman named Sacagawea, or Bird Woman.) In a single vertical mile there may be four jay territories, each inviolate, bound only by elevation above the sea. To travel well within your neighborhood, said Samuel Johnson, is the greatest of journeys.

*

I work at a university perched on a high bluff over the Willamette River. Across the river is a line of velvet hills punctuated by soaring hawks; below the campus is the sinuous gleam of the river, a waterway for creaking flotillas of great blue herons. The campus itself is a village of many species: students, professors, employees, cars, insects, trees, birds. Students and birds are the most exuberant. The students chirp, preen, molt, congregate in gaggles and flocks, perform bizarre courtship dances. The birds study insects, analyze traffic patterns, edit lawns, flutter through classrooms. Some birds live in residence halls; others commute to the university. I have seen nests in eaves, nests in pipes, nests in windows.

The office where I type these words was an empty attic corner two years ago. Where my fingers rise and fall there was a pigeon nest. Perhaps there has been life in this corner of the building since 1891, when it was built. One year it stood empty and there were goats in the halls. Then this floor was a dormitory filled with boys. Then it was a biology laboratory filled with animals and insects. Then it was a place where the wind lived. Now I live here on weekdays, and under the window where there were pigeons there is me, writing about birds, my fingers fluttering.

*

In the ancient days of falconry, according to the abbess Juliana Berners, there was a hierarchy of bird possession: eagles were for emperors, gyrfalcons for kings, peregrine falcons for earls, merlins for ladies, goshawks for yeomen, kestrels (sparrow hawks) for priests, and muskets (woodland hawks) for altar servers. Those days of yore were the halcyon days of falconry, the art by which raptors are trained to the hand. Probably this ancient art began as a means to procure food, but by the abbess's day falconry was a pastime fully as ritualistic and as filled with lore as any religion, and the reaping of rabbits and birds for the pot was incidental to the training and flying of the hawks themselves. No craft of the medieval ages was as respected, and none led to as many arguments about the best way to practice the art. It was King James I, the fellow for whom the King James Bible is named, who noted that falconry was an extreme stirrer-up of passions. "That is because the hawks themselves are furious creatures, and the people who associate with them catch it," wrote T. H. White, whose book *The Goshawk* is both meditation on the poetry of raptors and modern manual for their training to the fist.

Of all birds I love the raptors best. They are the most dramatic, the largest, among the most intelligent. Falconers say that raptors are fully capable of love, hate, and violent emotional instability. They are creatures that veer wildly from love to hate, that eat their fellow creatures, that soar in the sky and squabble in the mud, that care tenderly for their infants and battle with their adolescents, that reportedly can love, lust, laugh, play, mourn, wage war, speak a language, and endure depression.

I think that they are my cousins.

*

We eat birds. We have eaten them for many thousands of years. Chickens, pheasants, game hens, sparrows, pigeons, doves, quail, chukars, turkeys, hens, geese, grouse, ducks, larks. We have eaten nearly every bird that flies or swims or runs; it may be that we have eaten at least one of every species of bird. (Occasionally one *person* tries to eat every species of bird: King Richard II's menu for a weekend jaunt to his country home, in the year 1387, included 5 herons, 50 swans, 96 capons, 110 geese, 192 pullets, 240 cranes and curlews, 720 hens, and 1,200 peacocks.)

Birds die for us by the billions. They become feasts, cures, salves, sandwiches, soup. Their bodies stave off our hunger and sadness. The writer M. F. K. Fisher told the tale of the Maréchal de Mouchy, who returned home from the funeral of his best friend and ordered two roast pigeons for dinner. "I have noticed that after eating a brace of pigeons I arise from the table feeling much more resigned," he said to his cook. His cook, if frugal, probably took the remnants of the roast birds and made soup, perhaps to succor a sick child, perhaps to savor on a cold winter afternoon, when all seemed bleak and dead, and steaming soup could lift the heart.

*

They *fly*. They go where we cannot go. They lift themselves into the air and dream away. A simple process: weighing next to nothing, hollow boned, with lung capacities a hundred times greater than ours, they swim into the air and stay there, their wings marshaling what poet William Blake called the First Element. Their wings are curiously human in bone structure: the outstretched arm of an albatross could be that of a basketball player—humerus, radius, ulna, carpus, hand, fingers. A biology professor friend of mine told me she always used birds as examples when teaching

bone structure. No other creature, she said, made such an immediate impact on students. Once in a while she would notice a student surreptitiously extend his arm like a wing, seeing his own
appendage with new eyes, flexing his fingers up like a hawk surfing a thermal.

*

They are what we once were: vigorous creatures fully immersed in
the physical world. For better, I think, human beings long ago
grew out of that immersion and strove toward a different world,
one of reason, one of the spirit. But we do well when we pay attention to our forebears, who are exuberant; we do evil when we cast
them aside as appendages, servants, underlings, tools. We are ourselves underlings to something vast, and a scrabbling for power
among servants is a battle of children in dust.

In them is poetry, energy, joy; in them is life, pure and untram-
meled, unadulterated and holy. We learn most and best about life
by contemplating life; that is why we stare achingly at our children as they sleep, that is why our happiest moments are those
spent in the arms and hearts of those who love us, that is why we
are inexplicably pleased when a sparrow pauses for a second at the
window and regards us with an irrepressible eye. Small as she is,
she is our teacher and our companion, our fellow tatter torn from
the cloak of the Maker. She is a small vigorous prayer, a hymn
with wings, a smile given life and set aloft.

Glory Bee

I had the rare pleasure recently of a private Mass; that is, a Mass at which there were only two people, not counting Christ, who arrived during the Eucharist. There was the priest, and there was me.

Outside the room there were two sparrows also, and inside the room, it turned out later, was a bee. I believe it was the common honeybee, *Apis mellifera,* and not one of its cousins, *Apis dorsata, florae, cerana,* or *laboriosa,* but I didn't get close enough for an especially good look and neither did the priest.

The Mass was in a room in a residence hall at a college because neither the priest nor I had been able to find a Mass being said elsewhere during a day on which we had been thrown together in the social ramble, and as neither of us wished to go a Sunday without spiritual sustenance and the nutritious central ritual of our faith, we found a room in a residence hall, and the priest, as he said, found the materials necessary for him to say Mass, and so he did.

The bee lifted off from a windowsill just as the priest finished preparing his cruets of water and wine and opened his book to begin Mass. It began to fly due north, toward the table where Mass was about to commence, and it did not fly in a straight line, but in a series of short zigzags, not unlike repetitive dance steps. It is interesting to note in this regard that *Apis mellifera*, like all honey-bees, conducts a dance to inform its mates of food sources. There are three dances: the round dance, the sickle dance (used only by the Italian race of *mellifera*), and the waggle dance. The dances may indicate meals as far away as a thousand meters.

The meal of the Mass began. Opening prayers, first reading, second reading, the bee was still aloft, Gospel reading, the bee subsided, the creed, intercessions, the bringing forth of the gifts by yours truly, the bee was up, communion, the bee was down, con-cluding blessing, the bee was up, the Mass was ended, the bee was down, go in peace, the bee was cutting dance steps in the air.

The words that hung in the air with the bee were powerful and spare, as simple and sweet and dangerous as the bee, as potentially painful and penetrating, like nails through palms. The priest sang and chewed the words as if they were poems, which they are, and I heard them as if for the first time, my mind circling and wag-gling, remembering the days many years ago when I was a child standing in a church with the Mass washing over me like a sea of sound, a child picking up a fallen word here and there; and from these spent beautiful bees falling around me, *Apis mellifera* in the autumns of their days, words falling on the pews on the floor on the shoulders of the men and women around me, I built a story about the Mass, about sweet stinging Christ, about the God I heard and smelled but could never see, about believing against all reason and rationality that at one time God showed his sad radi-ant brown bearded Judean face and danced upon this earth and put Aramaic words into the dusty air—and then I heard other stories and stitched them into my story too, and then after many years I was standing in a room after a private Mass and I was

thinking that the Mass, stripped to its bones, is a fiercely persistent memoir, a naked meal for a naked carpenter, an act of exuberant joy that he lived and died and lived. How apt that this
Mass be said over a circling bee and two birds as well as one stung
man: for the Mass brings all creatures together in and under the
Word, which was in the beginning, which has no end, which will
always bee.

Crushing a Car

My first car was a useless 1977 Chrysler LeBaron, as mean and obtuse a car as ever existed. We fought for years and then it was crushed by a man named Toady. He towed it behind his shop and crushed it in a portable crusher. The crusher squatted on a flatbed truck like a frog on steroids. In the space of five seconds the LeBaron was reduced to a steel mattress thirteen feet long, five feet wide, and six inches high. Toady sandwiched this curious object with four other very flat cars for a trip to the shredder. After the LeBaron was shredded, he said, it would be melted into a steel brick. The brick would then be sold to make a bridge or a car.

Toady was a burly man with a crewcut and one bad eye. His left eye was honest but his right eye kept going off on its own in a vaguely circular pattern. I found it hard to concentrate on the fate of my LeBaron, which had cost me a lot of money and run smoothly for about a week. Soon after I bought the car I bought a very cheap tape deck for it. The tape deck worked properly for about a week too. It developed a heart murmur and lost one of its two knobs when a furious girlfriend kicked it to death with her red high-heeled boots. By chance it had been set on a country station when it was attacked, so it never played any other music but the haunting melodies of America's vast sadness.

The LeBaron broke down in nearly every town in New England. For a while it broke down only in Massachusetts, but then one day it broke down in New Hampshire, and after that came the deluge.

Once it broke down in Maine not a mile from the gas station where I'd just had it repaired for nearly five hundred dollars.

"You just fixed this," I said to the mechanic.

"Well, it's busted again," said the man, politely. His name was sewn in red thread on his blue shirt:

B O B

I never met another Bob among gas station mechanics in New England, but I did meet John, Enzo, Angelo, Billy, Vikki, Vinny, Dave, and Simmie. The best mechanic among them, although I have no real means of measuring this, was probably Enzo, who sold fireworks, enjoyed digging up shards of Colonial pottery in his yard, and charged me the same amount no matter what he did to the car: $110.

It was Angelo who had the best sign over his garage: "We Specialize in Foreign and Domestic Cars." Angelo once repaired my friend Bill's car, a domestic. The problem was deep in the bowels of the engine, so Angelo removed a good deal of the engine. When he put it all back together again it didn't fit properly, and Bill could never get the car's hood closed again, although it ran fine. Bill never went back to Angelo.

I did, though. I liked Angelo, an exuberant fellow from Turkey. His garage smelled like my uncles, and his mechanics made rich muddy coffee that they offered to their customers with great pride. They were always glad to see me, and after a few visits they set aside a chair in the corner of the garage for me to read in. I read

Boswell's *Life of Johnson* in that garage one summer, in four long visits. Once Angelo came to tell me that the LeBaron was ready, but I was at the end of the book, when Dr. Johnson is very sick, and I wanted to read to the end, because by then I felt close to him and was sad to see him go. I remember that when I finished the book it was twilight, Dr. Johnson was dead, and the mechanics were waiting quietly for me in the dark auto bay.

*

Since the LeBaron I have had two cars, a Chevy and a Volkswagen. Both have been circumspect. The Chevy broke down only once in its life. This was in the middle of an apple orchard in Oregon. The car died as my wife and I were coasting down a hill. We slid slowly to a halt near an apple stand. I was in despair, sure that we would now be stomped to death by passing killers, sure that the car would never start again, sure that we were doomed to spend the rest of our days in this forlorn orchard, probably with ice picks in our heads.

My wife, however, was not displeased that we had broken down, as the apple stand was open. She jumped out and bought several bags of freshly picked apples. At the time she was enormously pregnant and could not carry much else but the baby, so a parade of helpful people carried the bulging bags of apples to the car, where I was sitting with my head in my hands, thinking about ice picks.

"Is your husband all right?" asked a gaunt apple man.

"He's okay," said my wife. "He just thinks the car will never start again."

"We'll jump him," said the man, curtly. The hair rose on my head. But he brought back jumper cables and hooked them up to his tractor and electrified us and we drove home, eating apples.

The car we have now, the Volkswagen, is a very fine car. It has started every time I asked it to, so far. Once it stopped running right in the middle of the road, causing me great despair, but it turned out that we had run out of gas. My wife recognized the familiar signs of this malady. "I've run out of gas plenty of times," she said, airily. She was less airy two hours later when I finished filling the tank with a gallon of gas that we'd gotten from a nearby station. We'd called a taxi to get to the gas station, and while I was splashing gas into a tank and on my shoes she was listening to the taxi driver, a man the size of Utah. He had a knife collection, a pistol collection, a snake he was trying to sell, and an intense interest in telling astrological fortunes by computer.

My wife and I drove home in silence. As we turned into our driveway at last, she spoke. "That man tried to sell me a snake," she said.

*

My friends' cars, in which I spent a great deal of time between the ages of fourteen and thirty, were representative of our itchy masculinity, general penury, and status as second and third sons in large families. Mostly they were onions handed down from above. At the low end were station wagons no longer serviceable as family buses; at the high end were now-flaccid muscle cars abandoned by older brothers gone to Vietnam, to college, and to careers as cops or firefighters.

The names of these cars are a swashbuckling poem: Nova, Skylark, Impala, Gremlin, Firebird, Fairlane, Corvair, Rambler. In them we rambled from town to town, beach to beach, bar to bar. We drank as we drove, we drank before we drove, we drank too much altogether, but none of us died in flaming car crashes. Friends of friends died, kids at our schools died, but we didn't die. When I drive now, with my elfin daughter belted into her car seat, her hands filled with gingersnaps, her mouth filled with song, I stare at the faces of other drivers, wondering which one is drunk, which one doesn't see me, which one will crash into me and take my daughter away.

A friend of mine named Dennis died in a flaming car crash recently. His car wobbled over the double yellow line of a Florida highway and hit another car head-on. Dennis was killed instantly. He was twenty-three years old. The other driver was killed instantly too. He was twenty-seven years old. It was about 2:45 A.M. when they died. Dennis was pronounced dead at the scene at 3:06 A.M. It was the day before Mother's Day. His mother, who had six sons, answered a knock on her door in Boston at 8:00 A.M. It was a local policeman who had known the family for twenty years.

"Ma'am?" he said.

"Which one is it?" she asked.

This remark stays in my heart.

*

My sister, now a Buddhist nun, had a car that refused to go faster than thirty-five miles an hour. This quirk fascinated mechanics and boyfriends alike. The car, a black Ford Falcon, lived long and prospered until one bitter winter morning when my sister got in, lit the joint in the ashtray, took a puff, and started the car. The engine block cracked in half, perhaps because there was neither water nor antifreeze in the radiator, and the Falcon died. I believe it was crushed.

Crushing a car, Toady told me, is a difficult task. Before the blow that flattens the car, there is the Draining Period, during which all fluids are drawn out. Then there is the Stripping Period, during which the car is shorn of all salvage—tires, mirrors, handles, antennae, oddly sized pieces of glass, interesting detail work, bumpers, radios, the engine, the gas tank. Then there is the Searching-for-Loose-Change Period, which may have been a ritual peculiar to Toady. He told me he averaged about two dollars per car, although he'd once had a ten-dollar car, an Oldsmobile 88. He also told me that small cars and beaters were most likely to be change producers, a fact that had sociological implications, in my view. Toady thought it a simple lesson: rich people didn't lose money on the floor, and poor people were more likely to be mishandling change in the car. "Big-car people break dollar bills and don't lose the change," he said, his right eye rambling here and there.

I had wanted to keep the LeBaron after it was reduced to a thick sheet of steel, but Toady didn't like the idea. "First off," he said, "I don't like it on principle. This ain't a gift shop. Secondarily, the thing is too fucking heavy. That's why your Japanese buy it, so as to make it into their cars, which don't weigh rat shit. What, are you going to put a fern on it? It looks like dog barf when we're done. Plus, what, are you gonna carry it home? You don't want to do this. Trust me."

Toady had the goods on me at the time—he had wanted to charge me to crush the car, and I had refused to pay another penny toward servicing the bastard, even for euthanasia—so I didn't argue. We bartered for its death; he agreed to crush it and I agreed to leave the right-front tire, brand-new, with Toady. I took from the car the one remaining knob on the tape deck. It was dangling crazily from its axle and was easy to remove: it popped off like a grape. I have it here before me as I write. It has a scuff mark at about two o'clock and a dent near noon. With its two concentric rings and web of scratch lines it resembles a bloodshot eye. I used to carry it with me as a sort of cautionary charm, its presence ritualistically defending me from my own stupidity, but later events proved that it had no power over a force of such size, and now I keep it in my desk, from which it jumps out occasionally when I move a sheaf of papers. Recently it leaped out when I was searching, God knows why, for the check I'd written for the LeBaron. Of such innocuous events are essays made.

Before I left Toady that day I made him show me other crushed cars. He crushed about a thousand a year. This was about average for a small salvage shop, he said; a big outfit would easily do two thousand cars a year. The array of former cars in his yard was astonishing. It was a museum of dead cars, a mausoleum of arrested motion. I remember seeing a few other Chryslers and feeling stupid about purchasing a car that was crushed so often, until Toady told me that he, like most wreckers, specialized in a handful of brands, so that he might then specialize in those parts. "You need Chrysler parts, you come to me," he said, proudly.

Right after that I noticed a former bright orange Volkswagen Beetle, but it turned out that Toady didn't specialize in their parts—he had wrecked the thing as a favor for his niece. The Bug had crumpled up like a paper bag, he said, and it made him leery of driving the little things. He had prevailed upon his niece to buy a Chrysler as her next car. "They're tough bastards, and I have parts," he said.

Since Toady crushed the LeBaron I am more attuned to dead cars, useless cars, car hulks in ghettos, cars with trees growing through them. I know of one Ford truck, in Oregon, with an alder tree growing through the cab, and I know a Ford Fairlane penetrated by an oak in the White Mountains of New Hampshire. I could also lead you to a DeSoto completely covered with blackberry bushes, near the Oregon coast, but winter wrens are nesting where the flywheel was and it does not seem right to disturb them twice. The first time I disturbed them they shot out of the car like souls freshly released from their bodies.

*

It calms me to drive. Perhaps this is a peculiarly American therapy, this racing along asphalt in a mobile living room. Perhaps it is the motion, the sheer forwardness of driving, that attracts us so; we seem to be accomplishing something even though we are only shifting scenes, letting the movie reel by. Outside the tinted window the documentary films fly past—desert films, mountain films, urban dramas, car chases. The soundtrack waxes and wanes. When the song ends we change tapes; when the car dies we get another and begin the second feature.

We eat, sleep, smoke, make love, make phone calls in cars. We bind our children to them with complex straps. We bathe our cars and oil them and give them drink. We drape black masks over their eyes. We plaster them with our politics and affections and obsessions, our emotions reduced to phrases suitable for reading at sixty miles per hour. We drive our cars off cliffs and into rivers and lakes; we leave them in the forest to be pierced by green things. We lay paths for them: dirt roads, gravel roads, asphalt roads, concrete roads. Asphalt is made of rock and oil and dust; concrete is made of cement and rock and sand. So we rearrange what is there in the earth to make carpets for our vehicles. We read magazines about them, attend shows where they are featured, clean them and feed them and bring them to a priesthood that ministers to them. Their priests and doctors speak a special tongue impenetrable to the masses. They speak of pieces and parts, hoses and tubes, but what they are really talking about is torque, power, fury.

The fastest I ever went in a car was 112 miles an hour, at about three in the morning on a flat stretch of beach highway in New York. I remember the uncontrollable shivering of the car (it was the LeBaron), the angry twisting of the steering wheel, the chattering of windows, the roar of everything. I remember my fear, which tasted like chalk. On the way home, at fifty-five miles an hour, I thought about the sudden swerve—for a rabbit, for a bird—that would have left me meat by the side of the road.

I see meat by the road every day on my way to work: opossums, raccoons, squirrels, cats, dogs, jays, sparrows, wrens, swallows, pigeons, snakes, chipmunks. Occasionally there is a crow or a vulture that didn't hoist itself up quickly enough to avoid a car. Here in the Pacific Northwest I see major meat by the road sometimes: elk, deer, antelope, even a cow once. Once I saw a doe splayed across the road in two pieces, a front and a back. The deer pieces were about twenty feet apart. The car that hit the deer was over-turned in a ditch. I stopped to help any men or women or children who might be in the car, but it was empty. It was a Subaru, I think, and there wasn't much left of it.

I thought a lot about that car over the next few days. I thought about how it would be towed away to a wrecker specializing in Subarus, how the wrecker would carefully drain and strip it and search its crevices for change, for the five-dollar bill folded into the glove compartment for emergencies, for the gingersnaps in a little jar for the baby, for the new sunglasses miraculously undam-aged. I thought about how the car would be crushed in five sec-onds by awful jaws bigger than the car used to be. I thought about how the car would be sandwiched with five or six other former cars to be shredded and smelted and sold, how it would then be melted into other cars or bridges or girders.

Essentially the same thing would happen to the deer. It would be towed into the woods, stripped and eaten by insects and birds and a bear, and melted into other creatures. A few trinkets would remain—a rack of antlers, a set of hubcaps. Nothing ever dies completely, and we melt into other creatures, leaving behind a story, a knob with a dent and a scuff, a pair of sunglasses, a mir-ror with the memory of your face, the ripple of syllables that was your name.

The Sudden Flight of Mrs. Wilhemina Kettell, in Summer

S ome years ago I was visiting the island where I used to live. My small wife and small daughter and I stopped to visit a former neighbor, Mrs. Wilhemina Kettell. She was seventy-eight years old and was growing smaller by the year. We all went walking on the beach with her enormous dog, Midas, who was growing bigger by the year.

Midas would not, or could not, ascend the beach stairs when we were finished walking. We huffed and strained to push him up. Finally Mrs. Kettell arranged herself above him and endeavored to pull him up. Annoyed, he shook his leonine head, and Mrs. Kettell rose suddenly from the stairs, described a lovely arc in the air, rotated 180 degrees lengthwise like a spiraling football, and landed on her back in the sand, about ten feet away. She was in the air perhaps two full seconds, and when she landed a little puff of sand announced her arrival.

My daughter, then age two, was the first to speak. "The lady is flying," she said.

Mrs. Kettell bounced up with no apparent ill effects, and we went on to battle Midas for another hour, to no avail, before finally she called the local minister of the United Church of Christ, the Reverend Hugh Knapp, who lived down the street and who arrived in seconds and hoisted the dog bodily over the seawall as if the creature weighed no more than a piece of paper. My former town is the kind of small New England sea village where the local minister is a strapping fellow, able to help haul lobster traps if need be, or caulk a boat, or winch a boat up from where it sits in deep water after a storm, although he has many other interests, and holds a doctorate from Yale, and plays the cello with verve and grace.

So our misadventure ended well—no one hurt, dog safe, muscular religion to the rescue. It is the sort of incident that may be remembered briefly as food for a joke but is eventually lost amid other and stronger memories, like the way Mrs. Kettell cared for her crusty husband, Mr. Prescott Kettell, on his deathbed, and the way her eyes light up when she talks about the old days on the beach when all the residents of Vernon Street met every Monday evening for cocktails, the hour for arrival being signaled by a blue flag run up the pole of one of the houses. On the flag were the letters *MECC*, signifying the Monday Evening Cocktail Club, which would convene at 6:30 P.M. on the dot and disband as the clock struck half past seven, that being the moment when the host's mother, Mrs. Fay, descended haughtily from upstairs, floating down the staircase like a queen, prepared for dinner to be served at that exact moment, as it always had been, as it always was, as it always would be. By the time she set foot on the first floor the house would be empty save her dutiful and slightly askew son.

Yet I wish to carefully record the flight of Mrs. Kettell in summer, because it was a lovely thing, sudden and beautiful, and the memory of my friend unexpectedly aloft, suspended against blue sky and blue water, stays with me. I don't know why, exactly. I believe Mrs. Kettell's flight was a kind of poetry: unexpected, poignant, direct, rhythmic. It had symmetry and lift. It had comedy and fear and the possibility of tragedy.

Tragedy would come later, as it always does, big or small; for instance, I just learned that Midas is dead. Mrs. Kettell wrote me a letter on yellow lined paper. Midas broke down system by system and after a couple of days Mrs. Kettell brought him to the veterinarian in the next town. The veterinarian said that Midas's kidneys no longer worked. Mrs. Kettell held Midas in her arms as the veterinarian prepared a needle filled with nepenthe. Midas lived for perhaps ten seconds after the injection and then his heart stopped.

In the normal course of things, back there on the beach stairs, Mrs. Kettell would have pulled once sharply, and Midas, her companion of eleven years, would have realized that his beloved mistress indeed wished him to ascend the stairs, and he would have done his best to accomplish this. We would all have repaired to her cottage for lobster-salad sandwiches and tea, and when the afternoon waned we would have, with real regret, kissed our neighbor and scratched the dog vigorously behind the ears and bundled ourselves off to other appointments, of which there would have been many, that being the nature of life, even on vacations, especially on vacations.

But no: Mrs. Kettell took to the air, and I am left powerfully moved by her flight. It was a matter of an instant, something unexpected and then gone immediately, like all poetry, like all love, and it was lovely beyond my descriptive powers, like the face of my daughter in the moonlight in her attic room, or the pursed lips of my two new sons as they search eternally for milk in the dark—as do we all, as do we all. I suppose we are all spiraling like footballs toward what we hope will be soft landings, but in this particular case the flight was presented in microcosm, an epiphany, a sudden performance, unadorned and perfect, something to remember, something to savor, like milk in the dark, like a cocktail on the beach.

Look: the lady is flying.

part five

Grace under Duress

I believe that even sadness and tragedy and evil are part of that Mind we cannot comprehend but only thank, a Mind especially to be thanked, oddly, when it is most inscrutable . . .

Leap

A couple leaped from the south tower, hand in hand. They reached for each other and their hands met and they jumped.

Jennifer Brickhouse saw them falling, hand in hand.

Many people jumped. Perhaps hundreds. No one knows. They struck the pavement with such force that there was a pink mist in the air.

The mayor reported the mist.

A kindergarten boy who saw people falling in flames told his teacher that the birds were on fire. She ran with him on her shoulders out of the ashes.

Tiffany Keeling saw fireballs falling that she later realized were people. Jennifer Griffin saw people falling and wept as she told the story. Niko Winstral saw people free-falling backward with their hands out, like they were parachuting. Joe Duncan on his roof on Duane Street looked up and saw people jumping. Henry Weintraub saw people "leaping as they flew out." John Carson saw

six people fall, "falling over themselves, falling, they were somer-
saulting." Steve Miller saw people jumping from a thousand feet
in the air. Kirk Kjeldsen saw people flailing on the way down,
people lining up and jumping, "too many people falling." Jane
Tedder saw people leaping and the sight haunts her at night. Steve
Tamas counted fourteen people jumping and then he stopped
counting. Stuart DeHann saw one woman's dress billowing as she
fell, and he saw a shirtless man falling end over end, and he too
saw the couple leaping hand in hand.

Several pedestrians were killed by people falling from the sky.
A fireman was killed by a body falling from the sky.

But he reached for her hand and she reached for his hand and
they leaped out the window holding hands.

*The day of the Lord will come as a thief in the night, in which the
heavens shall pass away with a great noise,* wrote John the Apostle,
*and the elements shall melt with a fervent heat, the earth also and the
works that are therein shall be burned up.*

I try to whisper prayers for the sudden dead and the harrowed
families of the dead and the screaming souls of the murderers but
I keep coming back to his hand and her hand nestled in each
other with such extraordinary ordinary succinct ancient naked
stunning perfect simple ferocious love.

There is no fear in love, wrote John, *but perfect love casteth out
fear, because fear hath torment.*

Their hands reaching and joining is the most powerful prayer I
can imagine, the most eloquent, the most graceful. It is everything
that we are capable of against horror and loss and death. It is what
makes me believe that we are not craven fools and charlatans to
believe in God, to believe that human beings have greatness and
holiness within them like seeds that open only under great fires,
to believe that some unimaginable essence of who we are persists
past the dissolution of what we were, to believe against evil hourly
evidence that love is why we are here.

Their passing away was thought an affliction / and their going forth from us, utter destruction, says the book of Wisdom. *But they are in peace. . . . They shall shine, / and shall dart about as sparks through stubble.*

No one knows who they were: husband and wife, lovers, dear friends, colleagues, strangers thrown together at the window there at the lip of hell. Maybe they didn't even reach for each other consciously, maybe it was instinctive, a reflex, as they both decided at the same time to take two running steps and jump out the shattered window, but they *did* reach for each other, and they held on tight, and leaped, and fell endlessly into the smoking canyon, at two hundred miles an hour, falling so far and so fast that they would have blacked out before they hit the pavement near Liberty Street so hard that there was a pink mist in the air.

I trust I shall shortly see thee, John wrote, *and we shall speak face to face.*

Jennifer Brickhouse saw them holding hands, and Stuart DeHann saw them holding hands, and I hold on to that.

Kaddish

Kaddish L'anashim

The man who just liked to read the newspaper quietly
The man who loved to preserve tomatoes
The man whose two-year-old son is mortally ill
The man who slept with his two dogs
The man who occasionally vacuumed his lawn
The man who was building a dollhouse for his daughter
The man who was assistant treasurer at his church
The man who helped found a church in New Jersey
The man who was the best probationary fireman ever
The man who built tiny ceramic railroad towns for his daughters
The man who built forty crossbows
The fireman who died with his fireman son
The fireman who died with his fireman brother
The fireman who died with his policeman brother
The fireman who ran in with his fireman brother who survived

The fireman who hugged his fireman brother before entering
  the tower
The man who had ten children, the youngest an infant
The man who loved Cole Porter
The man who loved Bruce Springsteen
The man who loved Abba
The man who loved The Who
The man who was identified by his Grateful Dead tattoo
The man who loved model trains
The man who loved surfing
The man who loved the Denver Broncos
The man who loved the Detroit Lions
The man who loved his racehorses
The man who loved to run at night
The man who loved to fish for striped bass
The man who fished for bluefish from his lawn
The man who loved his boxer dogs
The man who loved fine red wine
The man who loved Stolichnaya vodka on the rocks
The man who loved skyscrapers
The man who loved birdhouses
The man who loved Les Paul guitars
The man who loved dominos
The man who loved comic books
The man who was rebuilding a 1967 Mustang
The man who rebuilt a 1967 Mustang
The man who was rebuilding a 1948 Studebaker
The man who was rebuilding an MG convertible
The man who restored an old hotel
The man who started a ska band
The man who built harpsichords
The man who had been a model
The man who could ski like the wind

The man who drove a taxi as a hobby
The man who drove blind women to church on Sunday
The man who delivered papers every morning before going to
    work as a cook
The man who meticulously rotated the socks in his drawer for
    even use
The man who liked to handicap horseraces
The man who wasn't a saint by any means according to his mom
The man who was the youngest county treasurer in Missouri
    history
The man who liked to cook kielbasa
The man who liked to cook pinto beans
The man who liked to cook meatloaf
The man who liked to paint his daughters' fingernails
The man who made a thousand paper cranes for his wife
The man who made tea for his wife every day
The man who cooked for his blind mother as a child
The man who had his mom's name tattooed on his arm
The man who had a bulldog tattooed on his arm
The man who had Death Before Shame tattooed on his arm in
    Gaelic
The man who really wanted to go to Egypt
The man who had been a boxer in Britain
The man who had been a private detective
The man who had been a cricket star in Guyana
The man who had been a basketball star in the army
The man who had been a lacrosse star in Australia
The man who had been a lacrosse star in America
The man who had been a hockey star in Canada
The man who had been a hockey star in America
The man who was an expert surfer
The man who carried a surfboard everywhere
The man who was a quadriplegic and typed with his mouth
The fireman who played the bagpipes

The fireman who played the piccolo
The fireman who played the pennywhistle
The man who made tea and toast for his wife every morning
The man who hung out the flag with his daughter every
    morning
The man who made wine in his basement
The man who knew everything about boats
The man who fixed his son's toy boat in the basement the night
    before
The man who liked to quote Federico Fellini about the passion
    of life
The man who was slowly going blind
The man who bought bagels for everyone all the time
The man who tied fly-fishing flies with his daughter
The man who drew cartoons and caricatures of his friends
The man who went to thirty-five Bruce Springsteen concerts
The man who went to Mass every morning before boarding the
    train
The man who cared for his kid sister who had cerebral palsy
The man who was a minister at House of God Church
    Number 1
The man who was an elder at the Kingdom Hall of Jehovah's
    Witnesses
The man who served two kinds of caviar at football tailgates
The man who mounted a telescope on a sewer pipe in his yard
The man who was married in full Scottish regalia
The man who spoke Portuguese at home so his children would
    know the language
The man who carried an old lifeguard from his wheelchair into
    the ocean for a last swim
The man who carried a woman and her wheelchair fifty floors to
    the street
The man who was deaf and had been a furrier in the old country
The man who was deaf and knew everyone in town

The man who sat with the girl no one liked in high school
The man who invited a mentally retarded girl to sit at the
    football players' table
The man who flew small airplanes on Sunday mornings
The man whose first son was born the day after he died
The man whose first son was born a week after he died
The man whose first son was born two weeks after he died
The man whose first son was born three weeks after he died
The man whose daughter announced her engagement two days
    before he died
The man who wrote a song about noodles with his daughter
The man who cleaned his neighbors' gutters
The man whose parents were deaf
The man whose parents survived the Holocaust
The man whose identical twin survived
The man who once painted his black dog white
The man who was a professor of geography
The man from Cut Bank, Montana
The man who dressed up like Elvis for his daughters
The man who wanted to coach high school basketball
The man who wanted to be a fly-fishing guide in Montana
The man who shoveled snow for his pregnant neighbor
The man who shoveled snow for old neighbors
The man who called his mother every morning at nine sharp
The man who called his father every day after his mother died
The man who called his wife three times a day
The man who called his wife every day after lunch for fourteen
    years
The man who left notes on the breakfast table every morning
    for his son
The man who fixed a television transmitter with his shoelaces
The man who coached every baseball player in his town for ten
    years

The man who was working overtime to save money for his
    daughter's birthday
The man who met his wife at a production of *Romeo and Juliet*
The man whose wife found out she was pregnant after he died
The man who helped his wife down eighty-eight floors and then
    went back in
The man who boated down the Mekong River
The man who rescued children from a daycare center that
    morning
The man who rescued infant twins from a burning building
The man who rescued an elderly couple from a burning building
The man who carried a man from a burning building
The man who carried a woman down seventy flights of stairs in
    the 1993 bombing
The fireman who carried a paralyzed child on a tour of the
    station house
The man who delivered a baby in an ambulance
The man who carried toys with him for distraught children on
    his paramedic calls
The man who carried dog biscuits in his pockets everywhere he
    went
The man whose dog cried all night long for two weeks afterward
The man who mowed the Little League field with his own
    lawnmower
The man who had just taught his son to whistle
The man who taught his pet bird to whistle
The man who had just taught his daughter to dribble a
    basketball
The man who had just signed up for his first college class
The man who went to college classes every night
The fireman who was also a substitute teacher at the junior high
The fireman who accidentally burned down his own firehouse
The man who wore photographs of his children on a necklace

The man who still did cannonballs when he jumped into the pool
The man who had been homeless for years but finally had a job
The man whose job started the day before
The man whose job started two days before
The man who started his own carpet-cleaning company
The man who grilled ribs in winter while wearing a parka
The man who loved to catch crayfish in his creek
The man who raised racing pigeons
The man who carried his failing wife everywhere in his arms
The man whose police shield is in President Bush's pocket

Kaddish L'nashim

The woman who loved her two dogs
The woman who loved her three dogs
The woman who loved really strong coffee
The woman who was a firefighter
The woman who loved to ride her bike in the desert
The woman whose job started the day before
The woman whose name meant *love* and *joy* in Yoruba
The woman whose sons were named Oz and Elvis
The woman who raised llamas
The woman who taught karate to deaf children
The woman who taught every Sunday at Holy Rosary School
The woman who had piercing hazel eyes
The woman who had a famous giggle
The woman who sang lead soprano at church
The woman who played piano for opera troupes
The woman who loved dancing to the Violent Femmes
The woman who loved everything British
The woman who fought the bully in school
The woman you could count on for anything
The woman who was raised by missionaries in Japan
The woman who had prayed the rosary with the pope

The woman whose son is autistic
The woman whose identical twin survived
The woman who had been homeless
The woman who brought clothes to homeless mothers
The woman who died with her nephew
The woman who died with her brother
The woman who died with her husband and brother
The woman who had toured the country singing with Duke
     Ellington
The woman who wanted to open a flower shop
The woman who collected angels
The woman who listened with her fullest attention
The woman who fed sparrows every morning in her backyard
The woman who gave her place on the elevator away that
     morning
The woman who was the craziest chocolate person ever
The woman who called her dad every day
The woman who loved pedicures on Saturday mornings
The woman who had just quit smoking
The woman who first kissed her husband under the twin towers
The woman who died with her husband on the 104th floor
The woman who had planned everything about her wedding
     except the invitations
The woman who wrote fifty-five-word short stories
The woman who wrote her will the day before
The woman who sketched commuters on the train every
     morning
The woman who was seven months pregnant
The woman who discovered that morning that she was pregnant

Kaddish L'yiladim v'yiladot

The boy who wanted to be an ambulance driver
The girl, age four, flying with her mother

The boy, age three, flying with his parents
The child inside the woman who was seven months pregnant
The children inside mothers who didn't know of them yet
The children who would have been conceived in years to come
Their children, and their children's children
May they swim in the sea of the Lord forever.

His Sweet Weight

When someone dies we mourn the loss of his verve and the stilling of his body but not so much the way he occupied space; so I sing Tommy Crotty, who was a graceful man, seventy inches tall, murdered on the morning of September 11 in New York City.

His foundation was built in 1958 by the firm of Patricia and Thomas Crotty Sr., formerly of Brooklyn. The final touches to his structure were completed by 1976, and it was an enduring regret to him at that time that he could go no higher, for he was a very fine basketball player, and forwards like myself, all of two inches taller, looked down on him as a species of Guard, which is to say a selfish and weak entity, content to hog the ball and fling it wildly from safe distances and never venture into the meat market of the lane; but Tom turned out to be the best and worst kind of guard, for he shared the ball relentlessly, a great virtue, and he was a greedy hawk on defense, a great vice, for he stole our awkward dribbles and fitful passes and caused ruckus and dismay among our fearful knees. He was never still, always had the ball, zoomed around larger players, never lost his temper, grinned a small grin, was never the star but always the fulcrum of control and change. He never seemed to hurry but he never seemed to be at rest either—an odd dynamic, a sort of relaxed perpetual motion.

This stays with me.

I went my way and he went his and here and there we would cross paths when back in our home village—after Mass, perhaps, or at someone's mom's funeral. I'd hear his name over the family table, over coffee on the porch, over beer at the beach: Tom becoming a high school star (Tommy *Crotty?*), Tom making the Long Island all-star team (which *always* picked flashy guards, never workmanlike forwards), Tom earning a scholarship to Marist College upstate (*college* ball?), Tom going into finance, Tom getting married (someone married *Tommy?*), Tom and his wife having daughters, Tom working at Sandler O'Neill on the 104th floor of the south tower of the World Trade Center.

Remember the way he scuttled up and down the floor with the ball?

Yeh—his brothers played like that too, like they were crickets on caffeine . . .

But then one day I am reading the stories of those who are lost, those who are fine gray dust being breathed all over the city—the brothers who washed dishes at Windows on the World, the best aunts in the whole world, the fireman who hilariously cut hair, the boy age eleven flying alone nervous excited to California, the baby from Boston, the priest crushed by debris as he sent a fireman's soul aloft, the man who loved ceramic eagles—and I see

Crotty, Thomas Gerard, 42

and I *see* him swerving along with the ball, sweating gently, wheeling around a pick, whipping a pass inside without stopping his dribble, the meat who gets the ball lurching to the basket and scoring, Tommy grinning (*the meat scored!*) and smoothly, almost lazily, sliding back upcourt, and then I see his wife sleeping alone in their bed, her hands remembering his sweet weight, the smile of his space.

So what prayer can I speak into the jagged wintry hole where Tommy Crotty used to be?

Only that little grin as he spun to go upcourt; only the fluid way he spun; only memory as a prayer against murder; only a snarling conviction that the men who murdered him must face him; only an unshakable conviction that who he is can never die, no matter how hot the fire.

Last Supper

E mmet's last supper with us was lamb stew, simmered all after-noon with white beans and garlic and tomatoes and oranges, served with spinach salad and freshly baked bread, accompanied by a red wine from Tuscany. He sang; he told stories. He kept his jacket on during dinner because he was cold, although it was a warm spring evening just after Easter. He removed his fisher-man's cap during the meal but put it on again when the dishes were cleared; he was cold, cold. He sang in Gaelic; he sang in English. He sang a song about a mother's love for her children and he sang a song about a whiskey jug. He said grace to open the meal and blessed my daughter after the meal, placing on her head the same huge hand that had baptized my sons two years before at the very same table, the boys cupped in that gentle slab like fish in a sweet net.

He was very sick then, chilled with the cancer that would soon kill him, with the knowledge of it eating him as he ate the lamb, and he was weak—he had toppled slowly into the ocean of ivy around my house when we arrived, and lay there for a moment like a fallen fir, smiling—but he savored his supper like a starving man, and sipped a little wine in honor of his friend Christ, as he said, and his wit was quick and his memory rich, and when he stood by the door to go, his hand engulfing the knob, he sang a last song, in Gaelic, about calling in the animals at dusk. "I came in with a song and I'll go with a song," he said, and he did.

His last Mass, at Saint Michael's Church in Portland, was packed—people standing in the aisles, children perched on the shoulders of fathers. By then Emmet could barely walk, and he had to choose between standing long enough to say Mass or standing to serve the the Eucharist. He chose the Mass, summoning all the gas in his tank to hold the body of Christ aloft one last time, the thin wafer weighing a thousand pounds. After eating the Lamb himself he sat down in his chair, and while communion was served by others he beamed at the hundreds of people who had come to his last supper.

He died five weeks later, on a bright afternoon, called in by the Shepherd he loved so, the God he had served so long and so well with those sinewy hands and that silver voice, the God he swore was Irish, for who better to understand the people of the suffering road? And four days later he was buried in the coffin he had commissioned, of Oregon juniper from the high desert country, and so was laid to rest Michael Emmet Harrington, priest and storyteller, son of a son of County Cork, Emmet who was named for the rebel Robert Emmet, Emmet whose name meant "truth" in Hebrew.

I loved that man, admired the bone of his character and the expansive muscle of his heart, and I sing the long strength of his love, now flung abroad to all the waters and woods of the world. I say to you, Emmet my friend, the Gaelic words you said to all of us so many times, pausing at a door, the knob a knot in the net of your hand: *Go mbeannaí Dia thú*, God bless you, God keep you forever.

*

The priest died on a Monday and was waked Friday night, at his older brother's house. His funeral had been that morning, in the old cathedral, the archbishop presiding, and he'd been buried that afternoon in the city's main Catholic cemetery, Mount Calvary. The funeral procession wound up Mount Calvary along a road built by his father. His father had come from Cork as a teenager. All four of his sons had worked with him at one time or another, carving highways from the woods, laying roads through the city.

On a side table as you entered the older brother's house was the deceased's hammered-silver chalice, his black fisherman's cap, his tan walking cap, a loaf of fresh soda bread, a pound of roasted coffee beans in a redolent bag, his favorite soft long-sleeved cotton dress shirt, and a posed photograph of his parents, Big John and Blackjack Katie. John and Katie grew up six miles apart in Cork but met in America when Katie spotted John walking to work in the copper mines and said to a friend, "I'll marry that man," and did.

The dining-room table groaned with food, which the deceased had paid for, having left money in his will for that purpose: a last supper. Beer and wine were out in the backyard, and there was good whiskey in the study.

An old friend rose to speak of the deceased. The old friend is a priest in Montana. His father and the deceased's father were boys together on the coast of Cork. The friend told how their fathers had graduated from school at age twelve: they were coming home over the mountains from the market where they'd sold the families' morning catch, and they decided that it was high time for them to be graduated from school, and so they graduated, right there in the road.

Three of the deceased's young nieces did a step dance on the stones in front of the fireplace.

The priest friend unfolded himself from his chair again and said a poem and then told a story of a fire in Butte in which a Kerryman with wooden legs was caught: "His house was saved, but Dinny burned to the ground."

In a corner of the kitchen was an infant at the breast.

The deceased's older brother stood to thank the assemblage for coming to honor the life and memory of his brother, whom he had loved since they were new boys together. The deceased had been best man at his wedding, before the deceased was ordained, and that was the first and last time anyone had ever seen the deceased in a tuxedo.

On the side porch under a cedar tree a dozen men and two women smoked cigars.

A friend stood to read a short speech about the deceased that noted his enormous hands, quick wit, fluency in Gaelic, long patience, and silver tenor, which he used entering and leaving any domicile.

The local parish priest, a young man, spoke a long prayer and then led the crowd in a song—"Saint Brendan's Fair Isle," a rouser.

"Go mbeannaí Dia thú," God bless you, someone said.

"Thú? Is there Wicklow in you, then?" asked a second voice.

"Go mbeannaí Dia's Muire thú," God and Mary bless you, came the first voice.

"Go mbeannaí Dia's Muire agus Pádraig thú," God and Mary and Patrick bless you, said the second voice, and then both voices laughed.

The deceased's younger brother did a slow jig on the stones in front of the fireplace.

Three of the deceased's many nephews stood by the fireplace and eerily and accurately brought back the voices and gestures of the deceased and then of Big John and Blackjack Katie, the deceased's deceased parents, whom very nearly everyone in the room had known.

The Montana priest stood again and told a story about an Anglican bishop touring Cork. The bishop stops to chat with an old farmer, a Catholic. "Do ye have many Protestants here?" asks the bishop. "Not so many," says the farmer. "It's the rabbits are the worse pests."

The family counted how many of them had been baptized by the deceased: forty-seven. Number of family marriages celebrated by the deceased: fourteen. Number of family funerals: three—those of his mother, his father, and his youngest brother, dead too young.

A nephew accounted the deceased's professional career: teacher and dean at the local Catholic high school, principal of a second Catholic high school, director of education for the archdiocese, organizer for a Catholic education association, pastor at two large parishes. The deceased retired but three years ago and wished to spend his time on his bicycle and in the Holy Land and Ireland and Mexico, and reading and photographing, and eating long dinners with friends, and walking through the woods where he had fished and trapped as a boy, wild along the rivers during the summers his father cut a sinuous road through a deep fir forest as silent and huge as a green cathedral. He wished also to finish a scholarly project about the Mass rocks of Ireland, where hedge priests celebrated furtive Masses under the sharp eyes of the British soldiers enforcing the penal laws, and where the hedge priests were not so occasionally shot dead by soldiers. There was one such Mass rock in Ireland where the priest had been shot dead before he finished the Mass, and our deceased very much wished to journey again to Ireland and at that rock finish that Mass, so long paused—but he died.

The family counted how many of them were around the deceased when he died, five days ago: twenty.

By now it was past midnight. Children were draped on shoulders like scarves. People went home in bunches. The beer and wine came in from the backyard and the kitchen was cleaned. The food on the dining-room table was packed up and put away and given away on sopping paper plates. The deceased's possessions stayed where they were on the side table. The deceased's younger brother and sister embraced the older brother and went home. The older brother's wife, who had loved the deceased, went up to bed, and then a minute later so did the older brother, and that was the end of Emmet's wake.

A Prayer for Pete

The phone rings, it's an old friend, he tells me of another old friend who is dying. Our friend is in his forties, just married, with a little boy, and there's no hope, he'll be dead within a couple of years, and dying too in a most cruel fashion, piece by piece, as his body slowly fails around the bright light of his mind, leaving him trapped in the husk of what had been a wonderfully lithe body.

I try to imagine my friend inside himself, immobile in a dark crumbled castle, his mind racing—and I have to get up and get outside and go for a walk.

So what prayer do I make for Pete? What do I say for his little boy, who will lose his father before he knows him well? What do I say for his wife, who will watch her new husband die a little every day and then be left alone with their son, who has the same thick red hair as his father?

I don't know.

Do I really think that my prayers will save Pete, or cut his pain, or dilute his fear as he sees the darkness descending? Do I really think my prayers will make his wife's agony any less, or reduce the confused sadness of his little boy?

No.

But I mutter prayers anyway, form them in the cave of my mouth and speak them awkwardly into the gray wind, watch as they are instantly shattered and splintered and whipped through the old oak trees and sent headlong into the dark river below, where they seem lost and vanished, empty gestures in a cold land.

Did they have any weight as they flew?

I don't know.

But I believe with all my heart that they mattered because I was moved to make them. I believe that the mysterious sudden impulse to pray is the prayer, and that the words we use for prayer are only envelopes in which to mail pain and joy, and that arguing about where prayers go, and who sorts the mail, and what unimaginable senses hear us is foolish.

It's the urge that matters—the sudden *Save us* that rises against horror, the silent *Thank you* for joy. The children are safe, and we sit stunned and grateful by the side of the road; the children are murdered, every boy and girl in the whole village, and we sit stunned and desperate, and bow our heads, and whisper for their souls and our sins.

So a prayer for my friend Pete, in gathering darkness, and a prayer for us all, that we be brave enough to pray, for it is an act of love, and love is why we are here.

Two Hearts

Some months ago my wife delivered twin sons one minute apart. The older is Joseph and the younger is Liam. Joseph is dark and Liam is light. Joseph is healthy and Liam is not. Joseph has a whole heart and Liam has half. This means that Liam will have two major surgeries before he is three years old. The first surgery—during which a doctor will slice open my son's chest with a razor, saw his breastbone in half, and reconstruct the flawed plumbing of his heart—is imminent.

I have read many pamphlets about Liam's problem. I have watched many doctors' hands drawing red and blue lines on pieces of white paper. They are trying to show me why Liam's heart doesn't work properly. Blue lines are for blood that needs oxygen. Red lines are for blood that needs to be pumped out of the heart. I watch the markers in the doctors' hands. Here comes red, there goes blue. The heart is a railroad station where the trains are switched to different tracks. A normal heart switches trains flawlessly two billion times in a life; in an abnormal heart, like Liam's, the trains crash and the station crumbles to dust.

There are many nights just now when I tuck Liam and his wheezing train station under my beard in the blue hours of night and think about his Maker. I would kill the god who sentenced him to such awful pain, I would stab him in the heart like he stabbed my son, I would shove my fury in his face like a fist, but I know in my own broken heart that this same god made my magic boys, shaped their apple faces and coyote eyes, put joy in the eager suck of their mouths. So it is that my hands are not clenched in anger but clasped in confused and merry and bitter prayer.

I talk to God more than I admit. "Why did you break my boy?" I ask.

I gave you that boy, he says, and his lean brown brother, and the elfin daughter you love so.

"But you wrote death on his heart," I say.

I write death on all hearts, he says, just as I write life.

This is where our conversation always ends, and I am left holding the extraordinary awful perfect prayer of my second son, who snores like a seal, who might die tomorrow, who did not die today.

In the Country of Fear

My furthest journey abroad, I believe, was the week I spent in a hospital two years ago, when surgeons opened my son's chest, cut and stitched among the highways of his heart, and slowly returned him to me. He is sitting across the room as I write, absorbed in a book about pigs, healthy as a horse; but I do not forget, cannot forget, our travels in the country of fear.

My son traveled alone, of course, a hard fate for a boy not yet two years old, and I have heard him talk of that time to his twin brother; and while I traveled with my wife and family and friends, each of us was in the end alone in that land. We were, in a real sense, abroad—not at home, but in a foreign nation, a country of unfamiliar topography and tongues, in an ocean of strangers, assailed by woes and wonders heretofore unknown. The woes were imaginable, if unbearable; the wonders were astonishing, and had to do with love.

I remember that I became hard of hearing in those days, and that food seemed less savory. I remember that I could never get physically comfortable, that I wriggled in chairs and waggled in bed, unable to relax or sleep. Being in that country was a kind of sickness, a seizure of the heart, and everything slowed excruciatingly. In the way of writers I kept notes, as a form of defense against horror, perhaps, and here are some: My son may be fine. My son may have some minor problems. My son may have major problems. My son may die. I try to imagine what it would be like if my son died. I cannot. I try again—try to envision a house where there is only one infant, one bottle, one stroller, one car seat, one boy. I cannot. When I concentrate on my writing I gnaw at my fingers, an unconscious habit for which I was often scolded in grade school by enormous nuns with faint mustaches and dockworkers' forearms. The scolding didn't take and I still chew my own skin, without thinking, when I am thinking. I eat myself. As I am thinking about Liam's death—about the way that his heart might stop on that glaringly bright table, under all those masked faces, under the lamps that are so bright they will make him cry, about how he might die a few nights later in the dark when his sliced and hammered body sighs and gives up, about how he might die a few years later on a sunny afternoon at the beach when a tube a pipe a duct a baffle a shunt a vein pops in his battered heart and that ferocious relentless muscle sags and the blood in his veins slogs to a halt and he falls to his pink knees near the water as his mother looks up from the porch and drops her book her tea her heart—I notice with a start that I am savagely eating myself and that my fingers are bleeding. The blood is a rich bright frightening red, the product of my perfect red heart. As bubbles of blood swell from the corners of my fingers I think suddenly of Liam's crooked gunslinger's grin, which starts out normally on the left side of his face like anyone's everyone's smile but slides down into a sly sardonic slice of merriment on the other side—and then slides into me like a brilliant perfect knife.

With His Hat
on His Head

A ll the rest of my life I will remember the young king kneeling at the deathbed of the old king, and the young man
weeping copious tears and holding his grandfather's big hand, and
the old king sprawling there exhausted, his skin melted back onto
the bones of his ridged face, his skin so thin and bright that it was
nearly translucent. He whispered his love to the young man and
peered at him with his fading grinning eye, and then he drifted
back to sleep, and finally in the evening he died, and so passed
John Bernard Harrington, born in the mountains when the world
was young.

One of the old Fianna of Ireland he was, a man fast afoot and
strong of arm, and he made cheerful war on the athletic field for
his university, and bitter war for his nation against the rising
empire in the East, and worked hard all his life to feed his family.
But he was a lovely storyteller altogether, *is bua na filíochta ag scoladh
as go h-aerach in ard a ghutha's a chinn*, his crafty stories leaping
from his throat, and many a time he sent me home grinning from

our chairs by the fireplace. Down the front steps and under the big cedar tree I'd go, smiling, thinking that here was a king of stories, a man with sweet words in his mouth, and when he leaned back and lifted those big bony hands and told his tales, the years fell off him like a cloak, and there by the hearth was the lithe warrior in the fullness of his strength, *súil dúshlánach agus anam dochloíte aige, 's a ghuaillí creagacha fiche troigh ar leithead*, with an impudent eye and a proud spirit and rocky shoulders twenty feet wide, as young and strong then, in the flickering firelight, as the young king, his grandson Joey, as celebrated now as his grandfather was in the morning of his days.

I have come to think that age cannot ultimately reduce a man, though it can inflict wounds, and cram pain into him, and feed him indignity, and rob him of those he loves, and finally kill him. But the mark of our maturity is how we carry our load, and this old king carried his with humor and grace. On a bright fragrant day recently he set it down and slipped away from those he loved, but who he was will live in my heart always: a man joyful and kind, with his hat on his head and a song on his lips. God rest him and keep the fire lit, the whiskey strong, the music quick, and Gaelic in the house.

part six

Children Are Verbs

*I believe that children are hilarious
and brilliant mammals . . .*

The Meteorites

The summer I was eighteen, hardly more than a child myself, I found myself ministering to a mob of boys, ages four to six, who ran like deer, cried like infants, fought like cats, and cursed like stevedores. They would eat nothing but jelly, and they ate jelly in horrifying doses: whole sopping dripping quivering plates of it, eaten swiftly with white plastic spoons, the spoons clicking metronomically against their teeth, the vast cacophonous dining room filled to bursting with small sweating children shrieking and gobbling jelly as fast as they could get the shrieks out and the jelly in.

There was David, who hardly spoke, and Daniel, who spoke for him, and who wept when he soiled himself once, five years old, too frightened to tell me his pressing need; David told me, quietly, touching me on the shoulder gently, whispering, "Counselor, Danny needs you." Daniel was the first child I ever wiped clean, and I believe now that when we stood together many years ago in a sweltering dirty toilet, on a brilliant August morning, amid fat buttery bars of morning light, Daniel sobbing convulsively as I washed him with a moist cloth, we were engaged in a gentle sacrament: Daniel learning that he must confess to be cleansed, me understanding dimly that my silence with this weeping child was the first wise word I had ever spoken.

There was Anthony, a tough even then, and there were his running mates, brothers who guarded their real names and went by Tom and Tim; and there was Lucius, a long lock of a boy, closed for repairs all that summer, unwilling to be touched, first to lash out, his fists hard as stones, his solitude and attitude dark as his skin. There was Miguel, age four physically, age fourteen emotionally, Miguel who fell in love with the ethereally lovely teenage girl who ran the arts-and-crafts room, Miguel who came to me one rainy morning and asked to be transferred from my army to hers. I conducted negotiations, traded him for coffee futures, and saw him only occasionally the rest of the summer, usually trailing in the scented wake of his love, sucked along in her sweet eddy like a lifeboat trailing an exquisitely beautiful ocean liner. Although once, late in a russet afternoon, just as the buses were pulling away in pairs from the parking lot and heading in the four holy directions with their squirming cargoes, I saw Miguel, alone, sitting in the front passenger seat of a bus, buckled in, hunched, sobbing— and for a moment, for all his eerie bravura and dash, he was a baby again, frightened and bereft. I was not man enough myself then to go to him, and I drove away and left him sobbing.

A sin: not my first, not my last.

There were Seth and Saul and Milton, who arrived together every morning in a large car driven by a silent man in a uniform, the boys spilling out of the car in a jangling wrangle, their gym bags intertwined like forest vines, the three of them inseparable yet apparently utterly incapable of affection. They argued all day long in their birdy voices, argued shrilly about balls and jelly and lanyards and swim trunks, about towels and mothers and thermoses, about sneakers and small gluey houses made of ice-cream sticks, argued all the way back to the elm tree where they waited late in the day for their driver, who never once opened his mouth, but drove up silently in the humming car, parked, emerged slowly from the front seat (unfolding himself in stages like an enormous jackknife), ushered the boys into the back seat (their reedy voices hammering away at one another like the jabs of featherweights), closed the back door (the camp air suddenly magically relieved of the shivered splinters of their tiny tinny angers), plopped back into the front seat (the fat dark leather cushions exhaling sharply with a pneumatic hiss), and drove away (the long dark car dervishing the roasted leaves of summer in its wake).

These then were the Meteorites, ten strong before we traded Miguel, nine strong on good days, which were days when David's mother let him come to camp. She worried that he was autistic, which he was not; he was just quiet to the point of monastic silence, except when it came to jelly orgies, during which he howled as madly as his fellows as the jelly was cornered and slain. In my first days in the maelstrom of that lunchroom, I raged at them as loudly as they howled at me; but then slowly I searched for silence, and by the end of the summer I had learned to sit quietly and watch the waves of sound crash on the sticky tables, slide halfway up the long lanky windows to the tousled forelocks of curtains, and recede frothing into the sea of clacking teeth from which they came.

*

Although I was by title a camp counselor there was no camp proper at the camp, which was actually a vast estate owned by the town and rented out in the summer. The estate house itself was enormous, labyrinthine, falling apart, very nearly a castle in its huge architectural inexplicability, and its unkempt grounds sprawled for many acres of fields, forests, and glades. Beneath the honeycombed house ran a small-gauge railroad that the childless owner had built for his nieces and nephews; it consisted of three cars, each about as big as a couch, and an ingeniously laid track that slipped in and out of the house and hill like a sinuous animal. The cars and track were, of course, expressly forbidden to campers and counselors alike, and so, in the way of all things forbidden, they were mesmerizingly alluring, and were filled every evening with counselors in various states of exuberance.

But the counselors in the railroad cars at night were only a fraction of the counselors as a whole, for most of us drove off in the afternoon in our tiny buses and vans, carting home our small charges and returning them sticky and tired to their parents. The buses peeled away two by two, large yellow rhinoceroses leaving the ark in pairs, and when they were gone the camp stood nearly silent in the long afternoon light, bereft of the bustling populace of the day except for, here and there in the forest fringes or sunning by the pool, counselors in entangled pairs.

Once, in all the years I was a counselor, I persuaded a friend to assume my bus route, and I stayed at camp until dark. I clambered up the stairs inside the house as far as I could go, and then I climbed out onto a roof and sat for hours, high above the tops of the oaks and maples that besieged the house below, watching summer turn ever so slowly into autumn. I remember the long bars of slanting light, the sighing and snapping of the metal roof as it cooled from the roaring heat of the day, the soaring of a bright brown hawk over the farthest softball field, the burbling of three pigeons astride a nearby roof, the redolent wriggles of marijuana smoke wreathing up from the archery yard, the faint sounds of voices far below me, under the house, in the tunnels. When the evening turned as brown as the circling hawk I climbed down, leaving the roof to the pigeons. In the deepening dusk I picked out the shapes of counselors against the hunched muscle of the trees, some running, some walking arm-in-arm, the only lights in the thick grainy twilight the burning ends of their cigarettes and joints, blazing pinpoints moving through the velvet dark like meteorites. I found a friend and hitched a ride home.

*

My first day as Lord of the Meteorites was utter chaos, in part because the boys were all wearing their names pinned to their chests on fluttering paper, and the papers flew off in the brisk early-summer wind, and the pins stuck the boys, and they stuck one another with the pins, etc. But things settled down over the next few days and we became easy with one another, as easy as a coltish and dreamy teenage boy can be with a mob of boys mere months, in some cases, from toddlerhood. We were for the most part interested in the same things—games, balls, hawks, bones, food, trees, hats, buses, songs with snickered words about functions of the body, the lovely teenage girl who graced the arts-and-crafts room and Miguel's dreams, the pool, and archery. They were absolutely *obsessed* with archery (although they could hardly handle even the tiniest bows, and even those bows mostly snapped emptily and whizzed over the boys' ducking heads when they tried to fire them, the arrows falling heavily to the ground without even a semblance of flight), and when they ran away from the march of Meteorites, which they did about once a week per boy, they could without fail be found in the archery alley, a broad grassy sward lined with stone walls, the whole grassy lane covered over by the high branches of sycamores, their fingers laced together in a dappled green curtain far above the lane, the fingers of the trees waving and sending down shifting flittering flitches of buttery sunlight.

My great fear as counselor was that runaway boys would head either to the pool or through the woods to the highway, but they never did, not once. To the bows they went like arrows, and I would find them there a little later, watching the patient and gentle archery girl show them, for the hundredth time, how to grip the bow, how to notch the arrow to the string (the arrow shaking badly, their eyes squinting, steamed glasses sliding down slippery noses), how to pull the curve of the bow back to their sighting eye (their soprano grunts like the hoarse chuffing of pigeons as they hauled on the little bows with all the narrow power they could muster), and how to loose the arrow with a flick of the fingers (a rain of bows in the air, a shower of arrows falling limply flaccidly to the summer earth, a comic ducking of boys as they evaded the thwanging winging bows). At that point I would emerge from the sycamores and reclaim my lost Meteorite, and back to the pack we would go, sometimes hand in sticky hand.

I don't remember that I ever scolded a Meteorite in this condition, for the archery girl was beautiful as well as preternaturally gentle, and the archery lane a peaceful island. Years later, when I had occasion to read a number of books about the Middle Ages in England and France, about castles and falconry and archery and knights and such, my mind continually and reflexively set the action in that quiet green lane, under the summery sycamores, on the lawn bound by granite walls, on that sward where bows flew and arrows lay face-down in the grass. For all the violence of sharp arrows knifing fat air and puncturing hay-stuffed targets, the archery lane was a wonderfully quiet place, and my mind wanders back there even now, in the chaos of my middle years.

*

The days of the Meteorites were in general circumscribed by geography. We were to be in certain places at certain times—the basketball court in the early morning (dew on the court, a toad or two, a silver shower jeweling from the net as I hit my first jump shot of the day), the arts-and-crafts room midmorning, the gym before lunch (the rubbery slam of dodge balls against walls, the clatter of glasses hitting the floor after a small boy is hit full in the face, the sail of his wail up to the ceiling), the softball field after lunch (languid, hot, ceaseless samba of cicadas), the pool (shimmering and cool and perfect, shrill thrill of whistles) and archery lane in midafternoon, and the basketball court again late in the day, for I was nominally the basketball teacher also, and so conducted ragged drills and motley scrimmages not only for the Meteorites, some of whom were barely bigger than the ball, but also for young Comets, Planets, and Asteroids (known to the rest of the camp as Hemorrhoids), as well as for the older boys in increasingly insolent waves, ending with my last class of the day, the Seniors, sneeringly fourteen and fifteen years old, some fully as tall and strong as their teacher, and one—only one, always one—angrily utterly absolutely determined to defeat the teacher in pitched combat.

This was Andy, Randy Andy, sniggering scourge of the Senior girls, Andy of the artfully tousled black hair and pukka shell necklace, quick fists and switchblade (carried for show), a charming suburban bully with bad acne, bad bladder (the boy peed on walls at least twice a day, marking his territory as regularly as a dog, leaving glistening triangles), bad attitude, a thug of the malls. Andy stole a bus, stole money, groped girls, smoked dope, came to camp drunk twice (a raw stench of beer and jelly rising from him on the steaming basketball court), shat on a chair on a dare, cursed the camp director, called his wife a fat whore, started a brushfire near the softball field, crucified toads to trees, beat a smaller boy bloody, and, hours after he struck out near the end of a counselors-Seniors softball game, carefully smashed all sixteen of the camp's bats to splinters—sizes twenty-four (Pee Wee Reese model) through forty-two (Richie Allen model).

I have sometimes imagined the dark poetry of that act, the camp silent after hours, Andy emerging from his hiding place in the vast warren of the estate house, stopping to pee against a wall, strolling smiling down through the gathering dusk to the softball fields, dragging out the dusty canvas bat bag from the equipment shed, standing the shrugging bag on end, selecting the Pee Wee Reese model (you want to start small before working up to Dick Allen's lumber), taking a couple of practice cuts (he had a lovely flat swing, as I remember), selecting a young oak to absorb the blow in its belly—and then the sick *crump* of bat barrel against tree bone, and the sudden green welt oozing into the oak, and then a second swing and crack and shatter as the bat explodes. He drops the splintered handle, shakes his hands to shuck the sting, and reaches for a twenty-six: a Luis Aparicio. And through the thin woods the sound of hammered vengeance echoes for almost an hour, and then dusk crawls over the scene, and then there is darkness.

*

Andy and I hated each other immediately, from the first minute we met, as he slumped against a tree and muttered a joke under his breath while I explained a drill to the restless Seniors. I was eighteen and nervous and so I got in his face, and from that instant— a windy and cold late afternoon on a dusty court in June long ago, our faces an inch apart, his blackheads marching from one temple to the other in an oily parade, my finger poking too hard into the tiny bowl of skin at the base of his throat—we were relentless enemies. And it is a mark of my own chalky insecurity and mulish youth that I hounded him every chance I got—reporting his crimes to the director, ragging him from the sidelines of softball games, catching his fist in midblow once by incredible luck (he was about to punch another boy for the second time) and so mortifying him before a girl, the ultimate humiliation for him and for me too, then. And now.

So every day at three o'clock when the Seniors slouched up to my court and ran my drills and halfheartedly scrimmaged and then circled watchfully and silently as Andy and I stripped off our shirts to play one-on-one, there was the entrancing possibility of blood in the air, and once there was blood on the asphalt, mine: he waited patiently for the right long rebound and the delicious angle of me chasing it headlong, and as I lunged for the ball he lashed his elbow into my mouth as hard as he could, and I bled. But I won, and his hate rose another notch. I remember the garlic taste of rage in my throat, and the tight taut circle of boys around us, silent, staring at the grunting players, the only other sounds the sharp shuffle of sneakers on dusty pavement, the relentless hammer of the ball, the dark anxious wind.

*

Flirting with the female lifeguards was a nearly universal and daily habit among the hundreds of male creatures at camp. The rare male counselor was he who did not detour his charges past the pool on their way to archery, art, lunch, gym, softball, basketball, or the buses home. Not even the camp director, an ebullient and brilliant con man named Buck, was immune to the lures of the pool. He arranged his office in such a way that his gaze naturally strolled out the open french doors of the house veranda and down a short flight of stone steps to the pool, and when he was not in his office (recruiting students *There is no camp on the entire north shore that can offer the recreational and educational amenities we can,* charming parents *I understand that Marc has been named camper of the week three weeks running, an unprecedented honor I may say and speaking of honor we would be honored to see you and Mr. Harrow at the annual Inner Circle dinner for special friends and benefactors,* chasing delinquent fees *I don't think you understand, Mrs. Kaplan; if we do not receive remuneration of your outstanding bill we will have to cancel Glen's pool privileges, which will come as a terrible blow to the boy,* evading creditors *My accountant tells me that the check was delivered yesterday via registered mail,* badgering vendors of food and gasoline and sports equipment and T-shirts *Yes, sixteen bats, various weights, you heard correctly, yes, there was an accident and an insurance claim has been filed,* writing camp advertisements and fliers *More than a hundred acres of fields and fun staffed by a hundred board-certified educators,* placating angry parents *I can assure you*

Mrs. *Steinberg that his counselor was with David from the minute the accident occurred until his arrival at the oral surgeon's office*, canceling social events *We will absolutely not have an end-of-the-year evening picnic for the counselors because last year it was a goddamned humpathon and one of these years we are going to be sued by some father over his daughter getting knocked up in that toy train*, judging art contests *How can I choose a winner when they all look like the kids spit paint on the paper?* disciplining counselors *Do you think this is some kind of dating service here?* hiring counselors *There is no camp on the entire north shore that can offer the recreational and educational amenities we can*, firing counselors *If I see you on the grounds ever again I'll report you to the police*, rooting impatiently through the overflowing lost-and-found box *If the catcher's mitt was so important why did you leave it in the lunchroom?* arguing with his wife *You told the Kaufmans their twins could come for free!?* flirting with his wife *What say we knock off early and knock one off?* checking his toupee in the mirror *Goddamned rugs*, cursing the estate's former owner for building *that damned railroad on which most of the so-called counselors at this camp spend their nights doing God knows what*), he was at the pool checking on *the insurance the floats the filter the schedule the chairs the emergency equipment the frogs floating there like turds in the morning* but really savoring the lithe bodies of his female employees. Because the camp sat high on a windy hill not far from the ocean, it was cold in the morning, even in July and August, and the lifeguards wore their sweatsuits until noon or so, and after a few weeks I noticed that Buck conducted all meetings and business in the morning, and hung around *checking on the crazy business of this camp* by the pool in the afternoon, when sweatsuits were off.

The geometric light of high summer, the sighing of afternoon winds through sycamore leaves, the shouts of giddy children in the shallow end, the cannonball geysers of older boys between the bobbined ropes, the streaming hair of Senior girls emerging blinking from the deep end, the sharp annoyed smell of chlorine, the

long lankiness of a boy unfolding midair from the diving board—
I remember it all now, my mind back in the itchy young cat-body
I had then, bouncing down the stone steps toward the pool, peel-
ing off my wet shirt, one eye on the shambling parade of
Meteorites following me like puppies, *Watch the steps, gentlemen,
the steps*, the other eye staring at the perfect alluring shadow
between the breasts of a girl in a bright-yellow bikini fifty feet
away. I take the last four steps in a casual easy bound and then lean
easily into the pool, shorts and socks and sneakers and all, and as
I go under I can hear the stunned hilarity of my boys and their
reedy voices rising in wild amazement: *Counselor went in with his
sneakers on!*

*

Of course I fell in love that summer, head over heels, led there by
the Meteorites, who watched me stare helplessly daily at one of
the lifeguards, a shy lovely girl, and then somehow conspired
among themselves to bring her to me one day, leading her by the
hand up the crumbling stone steps of the castle, up the balustrade,
down a sagging wooden hall lined with sagging metal lockers, to
our locker room, lined with sagging benches. I was slumped in the
corner, adjusting the bandanna I wore all that summer, waiting
impatiently for the boys to change into their bathing trunks (their
thin slippery bodies like the startling roots of plants just pulled),
when in walked Nancy, in her bathing suit, flanked by David and
Daniel, who led her by the hand toward me and then stepped
back, Daniel giggling, David not.

I was very startled; it was one of those few moments in life
when you are idly dreaming about a book, a place, a meal, a girl,
and you look up and *there she is before you,* smiling, her hair dry-
ing at the ends but still wet and tight to her head, one foot resting
on the other as she leans against a sagging locker, Daniel dancing
about like an elf, quite proud of himself, but David staring at me,

waiting for something. A look I would not see again for twenty years, until my own child, at the same age, regarded me as soberly, with such powerful expectation.

"Please sit down, here, sit here; move over, Lucius."

He glares darkly.

"I'm so seeprised to sue you here," I say.

Boys giggling at my tangle-tongue.

"The boys told me you liked me very much," she says.

My God.

"And I like you," she says. "Very much."

I, I . . .

"I, I've liked you for a long time," I say,

and with that we rise, as if rising simultaneously was what we had in mind, as if we had agreed on or arrived at something, and we collect the boys, Tim hiding behind the locker naked and frightened that the Lady might see his Penis, and we parade the Meteorites down the crumbling stairs and toward the pool, and somewhere on the stairs we hold hands, and so began that summer love, doomed and perfect, having much to do with sunlight and tongues, the taste of sunburned skin, car radios, bitter words on lawns, letters on loose-leaf paper, chlorine, bright yellow notes on the driver's seat of my bus at dusk, her college boyfriend, the clasps on a bra, the coy best friend, the mother's sharp eyes, the door of her room half-open, her shirt half-off, her face half-turned away.

*

The Meteorites are in their midtwenties now, college graduates mostly, I would guess, and perhaps at work, married, in prison, who knows? I have thought about them every summer—summer brings me the Meteorites, ten strong always, Miguel still one of us—but I have never made the slightest effort to find them, to see them again, however much they held my affections that summer, and I do not think I ever will. They would not remember me, and in their rangy man bodies, long boned, tending to first fat, I wouldn't see the lithe summer manlings they were. Yet I think of them more every year. I have small children of my own now, and I am surrounded again by hubbub and tears, comedy and fistfights, jelly and juice; and it is high summer as I write, the faraway shouts of children splintered on the wind, the smell of hot afternoon on my shirt.

But there is more than memory here, more than nostalgia, more than a man's occasional yearning to be the quick boy he was, more than a memory of a time that seemed timeless. I learned to love that summer, and not from the woman who came from water, although I loved her and she me, for a time, a month, a season, until the frost. I loved David because he loved Daniel, because David came to me that bright August morning and touched me on the shoulder and whispered, *Counselor, Danny needs you;* because while I cleaned Daniel, in that filthy hot bathroom in the thick morning light, David was waiting, his glasses askew, and when Daniel and I emerged into the clean sunshine the boys embraced each other, desperately, their thin fluttering hands like birds on the bones of their shoulders.

Counselor, Danny needs you, spoken in maple dapple by a small boy on a high hill, and the four words fell from his mouth and were scattered by the four winds: but they have been a storm in me.

Two on Two

Once upon a time, a long time ago, I rambled through thickets of brawny power forwards and quicksilver cocksure guards and rooted ancient centers, trying to slide smoothly to the hoop, trying to find space in the crowd to get off my shot, trying to maneuver at high speed with the ball around corners and hips and sudden angry elbows, the elbows of twenty years of men in grade school high school college the park the playground the men's league the noon league the summer league, men as high as the seven-foot center I met violently during a summer league game, men as able as the college and professional players I was hammered by in playgrounds, men as fierce as the fellow who took off his sweats and laid his shotgun down by his cap before he trotted onto the court.

I got hurt, everyone does eventually; I got hurt enough to quit, back pains then back surgery then more surgeries; it was quit or walk, now I walk.

174

The game receded, fell away, a part of me sliding into the dark
like a rocket stage no longer part of the mission.

Now I am married and here come my children: my lovely dark
thoughtful daughter and then three years later suddenly my
squirming electric twin sons, and now my daughter is four and my
sons are one each and yesterday my daughter and I played two-on-
two against my sons on the beautiful burnished oak floor of our
dining room, the boys who just learned to walk staggering across
the floor like drunken sailors and falling at the slightest touch, my
daughter loud lanky in her orange socks sliding from place to place
without benefit of a dribble, but there is no referee only me on my
knees, dribbling behind my back and trick-dribbling through the
plump legs of the boys, their diapers sagging, my daughter shrieking with glee, the boys confused and excited, and I am weeping
weeping weeping, in love with my perfect magic children, with
the feel of the tiny bright-red plastic ball spinning in my hands,
my arms at home in the old motions, even my head and shoulders
snapping fakes on the boys, who laugh; I pick up a loose ball near
the dining-room table and shuffle so slowly so slowly on my knees
toward the toy basket eight feet away, a mile, a hundred miles, my
children brushing against my thighs and shoulders like dreams like
birds; Joe staggers toward me, reaches for the ball, I wrap it around
my back to my left hand, which picks up rapid dribble, Joe loses
balance and grabs my hair, Lily slides by suddenly and cuts Joe off
cleanly, he takes a couple of hairs with him as he and Lily disap-
pear in a tangle of limbs and laughs, a terrific moving pick, I would
stop to admire it but here comes big Liam, lumbering along toward
the ball as alluring and bright as the sun; crossover dribble back to
my right hand, Liam drops like a stone, he spins on his bottom to
stay with the play, I palm the ball, show fake, and lean into a short
fallaway from four feet away,

ball hits rim of basket and bounces straight up in the air, Lily
slides back into picture and grabs my right hand, but I lean east

and with my left hand catch the ball and slam it into the basket all in one motion,

and it bounces off a purple plastic duck and rolls away again under the table,

and I lie there on the floor as Joe pulls on my sock and Lily sits on my chest and Liam ever so gently so meticulously so daintily takes off my glasses,

and I am happier than I have ever been,

ever and ever,

amen.

The Death of Rascal

He died during the night, alone, curled in the dark near the woodpile, where he had spent nearly all his life, and when the children found his body in the morning they wept. He had been so ill the day before that they had each visited him alone, in the evening, to say farewell, but in the morning when they found him dead they wept. The girl who owned him, if one creature can be said to own another, retreated to her room and closed the door. Of her two younger brothers, one could not be consoled and the other ate his breakfast in silence. When the time came for school the three children silently donned their jackets and gathered their books and walked up the hill to the bus. Their mother walked with them. When she returned to the house she dug a hole near the camellia tree, and her husband laid the animal to rest and she covered him with moist soil and heavy stones. They paused then, the woman and the man, staring at the little cairn, thinking of the short lives of pets, of the tears of children, of feeble explanations of death, of feeble explanations of the persistence of energy, of feeble explanations of soul and spirit, of feeble explanations of stories as potent prayers; and then they parted, she to her work and he to his, and so ended a hard morning for that family.

Yet the man kept thinking of the animal, whom he'd liked and often fed, the girl often forgetting to do so and growing annoyed when reminded, just as she grew annoyed when reminded to bathe the creature, and change his bedding, grimy tasks she detested and delayed. But sometimes she would bathe the animal in the kitchen, and he would explore the vast country of the towel, and venture to its borders, and sniff curiously at new smells, big smells, mysterious smells. Once the girl bathed the creature outside in the summer grass, and never was the animal so delighted, so inquisitive, so washed with bright air and new smells as that day; the only day the man had ever seen the animal squirm adamantly against returning to his place by the woodpile, the one place that was absolutely his, a place rife with the scent of cedar and pine and fir, and arranged in such a way that all children passing to and from the carnival of the basement paused there to pay their respects to Rascal, who rose to their salty fingers like fish to flies.

But he died, curled there by the woodpile, and we buried him by the camellia tree, and nothing I say to my daughter assuages her conviction that Rascal is utterly gone, his energy dissolved, his inquisitive spirit only a memory.

"His energy travels on in ways we don't understand," I say.

"But you don't *know* that," she says. "You only *believe* it."

"I believe it deep in my bones," I say.

"I don't," she says, and she retreats to her room and closes the door.

I have faith in his unlost energy and she has none, and this eats at me, for soon enough her grandparents will die, and a neighbor, and a teacher, and the sister of a kid on the bus, and a kid who used to be in her Sunday school class, and then eventually her father will die, before she does, if he is lucky (an odd blessing for which he prays daily).

Today Rascal, tomorrow everything else she loves, and if she cannot believe that who Rascal is somehow outlives what he was, how will she live? Without that hope in the intricate holy necessary stitching of life to death, how will she love?

Last year my wife went on a tree-pruning bender in our yard, reducing our trees to skinny naked skeletons of their former hairy exuberance. The camellia above Rascal was cut to the bone, and we thought it was dead. But a few weeks ago, out struggled green nubs that unfurled into gleaming mobs of leaves, and now the tree is thriving, albeit in different form.

So is Rascal—somehow.

But how do I teach that to my daughter?

Weal

I am rich in children, but they are driving me stark raving muttering insane. I think there are three of them, but they sprint
through the house and scream piercingly and slam doors and pee
in the bushes and break action figures at such a rate that I am not
altogether sure sometimes how many children or action figures
there are in the house. The children call me names and use bad
words and hide clothes under their beds and take their mother for
granted and get sick all the time and cough darkly on me and put
their muddy feet on the couch and throw mud balls at the house
and pour milk on the porch. They have broken two windows and
cracked a door. They have dug a pit in the yard big enough to trap
a car. They hide shoes in the freezer. They lose their homework,
their hats, their jackets, their backpacks, their tempers. Yet when
they are sick they drape themselves on me like warm shirts, which
I love, and they leave me notes sometimes in my shoes, which I
love, and they have honest loopy handwriting, which I love, and
now all three of them can read, which I love, and they read aloud

by the fire at night, which is the coolest sound I have ever heard, and when they hug me they hug me desperately and powerfully, and they murmur like small owls when they are sleepy, and they are hilarious twice a day, and sometimes, not very often, not as often as I would like, they turn to me and cup my grizzled face in their grubby hands and do the Vulcan mind-lock thing, their sea-green eyes drilling into me, and that is when I am most sure that I am a man wealthy beyond words in the only coin that matters, love, harried though it may be.

There are many shapes and forms of love, all of them slippery and nutritious, but to love and be loved by children is maybe the most complex and mysterious of all. In a real sense it is the bedrock of human persistence and culture, the sort of broad unconscious love we must rise to, or die choking in the world we have irredeemably fouled.

I try to keep this in mind even when the shrill shrieking in my house causes me to use bad words and hide in the basement.

Most of the people I love aren't dead, my work matters, and I see miracles all the time, miracles so consistent and mundane that I'm not stunned by them except when they are endangered, miracles like clean air and teachers and food, and nurses and laughter and light, and my wife, and a government still run mostly by its citizens, and the extraordinary grace with which most people carry their burdens. But the most miraculous of all our gifts is children; without them we would laugh less, we would be bereft of innocence, we would lose hope, we would shrivel and vanish, with no one to remember what we so wished to be.

Making the Bed

I am kneeling on the oak floor, hammering pine. My twin sons' twin beds have been delivered to the house by a humming man with braces. The beds are in many pieces. My wife and daughter and I must piece the beds together tonight so that the boys, already poured into their pajamas, can hit their respective sacks.

My sons are nearly three years old and the time has come for Big Boy Beds. The boys are poking each other with screwdrivers, losing the dowels for the beds, tearing the plastic covers off the mattresses, etc. My daughter, six years old, capable with tools and proud of it, is cheerfully screwing the wrong screw into the wrong hole in the wrong plank; but she does so with such diligence, with such concentrated chewing of tongue and cold-eyed appraisal of screw depth in screw hole, with such thoughtful arrangement of large muscles upon small tool, with such large joy in small task, that for once I hold my own tongue, and do not scold, or correct, or instruct, or lecture, or seek to correct her activities, but lean back on my haunches and watch.

My wife, a subtle woman, also watches in silence.

My daughter, absorbed, doesn't notice us watching.

She pauses in her labors, considers the tool in hand, lays it down, chooses another, sets to work.

I stare at her face. She's lean and long now, her baby fat long gone, her face brown from the summer.

It's been a tough summer—she's been rebellious, angry, quick to tattoo her brothers with her fists and feet, quick to bark and snap at her mother, to snarl at her father. Perhaps she is nervous about looming kindergarten; but perhaps too she is twisting the wrong way, growing not toward light but toward darkness. I worry about this daily. The rituals of her early years have slipped away, but nothing yet has replaced them; sometimes we read together sweetly and she folds into me like a new rib, but mostly now we don't, and often now we are sharp with each other, our voices have cutting edges, doors slam. Often I sit on the edge of the jail chair and try to explain my reasoning and she turns away; she says, "I don't care," she says, "I hate you," she says, "Are you finished yet?"

And often I sit there when she has stomped off and think, *What have I done wrong?*

I think maybe people of grace and courage and honesty are made like Big Boy Beds—piece by piece, slowly, with a lot of kneeling. I think maybe parents, despite appearances, haven't the slightest idea how to bring up their children, but simply keep at it with as much kindness as they can summon to the work. I think maybe we are making our children's beds all day long, year after year, until suddenly the child in the bed is a woman kneeling on another floor in another city making a bed for her child, and even then you don't stop making her bed, but lend a hand with the new bed too. So there is no end to the making of beds, including your own.

My daughter finishes her work and smiles broadly. We smile broadly. The boys, smiling broadly, hit each other with hammers.

Some minutes later, in my appointed paternal editing rounds, I come upon the wrong screw in the wrong hole, but for once I do not seek to correct the flaw, because it seems to me now that it is actually the right screw in the right hole, and we all build the rest of the bed, and although in the weeks to come my sons will continue to sleep curled on the floor as they always have, that particular bed seems like a wonderfully well-made bed to me.

Pop Art

In nine years I have been graced with three children and here is what I have learned about them. They are engines of incalculable joy and agonizing despair. They are comedy machines. Their language is their own and the order of their new halting words has never been heard before in the whole history of the world. They are headlong and hilarious. Their hearts are enormous and sensitive beyond calculation by man or machine. Their pride is vast. They are cruel, and move in herds and gaggles and mobs, and woe unto the silent one, the one who looks funny, the one who speaks awkwardly, the fat one, for she will be shouldered aside, he will never get the ball, she will never be asked to jump rope, he will not be invited to the pool party, she will weep with confusion and rage, he will lash out with sharp small fists. Yet they are endlessly kind, kind by nature, and among them there is often an artless democracy, a linking of arms against the vast puzzle of the long people. They search for rules and rank, for what is allowed and what is forbidden, and poke the rules to see which one bends and which is steel, for they wish to know their place in the world, where they might walk, what they may wear, which shows are allowed, how far they can go, who they are. They rise early in excitement and return reluctantly to barracks at night, for fear of missing a shred of the daily circus. They eat nothing to speak of but grow at stunning rates, producing mostly leg. They are absorbed by dogs and toast. Mud and jelly accrue to them. They are at war with wasps. They eat no green things. Once they learn sarcasm they use it with abandon, slashing here and there without control and wreaking havoc. When they weep they weep utterly from the marrows of their lonely bones. They will not speak of death, but when it comes, a dark hooded hawk on the fence, they face it without fear. They are new creatures hourly, and what you think you know of them is already lost in the river. Their hearts are dense books no one can read. They speak many languages of the body. To them you are a stone who has always been and will always be. When they are ill they shrivel. To father them is not a brief noun but an endless verb that exhausts, enrages, edifies, elevates, educates; I am a thinner and grayer man than I was, and closer to joy. They frighten me, for they will make a new world on the bowed back of the one I love; but they delight me, for to love them is to taste the furious love the Maker has for what he made, and fathers still, and always will.

The Measure of
Mystery

M y daughter and I are in the habit of reclining together in the
gathering twilight, in her small room at the top of the stairs,
in the last half-hour before she closes up shop for the night. Once
we are settled, coverlets and bears just so, there is the traditional
paternal quiz ("How was your day?" "Did you have fun?" "Where
did you go?"), the traditional daughterly replies ("Fine," "Yes,"
"Out"), and the now traditional paternal musing, there in the sifting dust of dusk, about the utterly mysterious interior life of my
oldest child, once a fixed entity the size of a shoebox, now a long-
legged unpredictability, Almost Six Years Old.

For some years now the last voice in Lily's ear every night has
been her father's baritone mutter, the guttural mumble of a man
shuffling through the published adventures of trolls, pigs, mice,
otters, wolves, and ballerinas. Some months ago we began a series
of invented tales about foxes, a story cycle that stars a small gray
fox named Phil who found his way into school one day and
stayed, a furry phenomenon in the last row. At our fictional Fox

Hollow School there are quizzes every Friday morning, and lately it has been Friday morning every night, as Lily has become absorbed by tests: science tests, spelling tests, math tests. Perhaps what she loves is the sense of accomplishment that comes with correct answers to questions like "How do you spell *door?*" or "Name three foods that a bear eats," or perhaps the startled pride in her father's gravelly compliment when his small student solves a conundrum like "What is eleven minus nine plus four?" Or perhaps it is simply that she loves the challenge, loves to measure her mind against mystery.

And lately, in that last lovely light, with that light lovely head on my chest, I have been mesmerized by the mystery of her mind. "How do you solve eleven minus seven?" I asked her the other night. "Easy," she said: "ten, one; nine, two; eight, three; seven, four; so the answer is four."

I puzzled over this for a minute until I saw the pattern, and then I lay there silent, overcome with the gift that had been given to me: the chance to watch a new mind flowering—and a mind, to boot, that I had begged the Lord for, ferociously, my fists hammering on his door night after night, until unto me there was born a daughter, a new note in the long song of the world, a story who will be told, I pray, long after I have myself become sifting dust at dusk. In the leap of her mind there is a miracle so startling that I am but a stuttering student of it, a small boy peering between the blinds, a child struggling to sense the Coherence in everything— and sometimes, just before nightfall, in a small room with a small girl, I do.

Yes

Lately I have been delving into early Irish literature and language, and so have been raiding cattle in Cuailnge, and pondering the visions of Oenghus, and feasting at Bricriu, and wooing Etain, this last of which has led to some tension with my wife, who is of Belgian extraction, and does not like to hear me tell of the beautiful Etain, the loveliest woman in all Ireland, although Etain was changed to an insect, and banished for a thousand years, until she was reborn as the wife of Eochaid Airem, king of the green lands.

I try to explain to my wife that I am only wooing by proxy, as it were, and that Eochaid has the inside track, he being in the story and me only reading it. This line of talk leads me inevitably to Flann O'Brien and Myles na gCopaleen and Brian O'Nolan, all of whom I wheel into the conversation, the three men standing all in the same spot, as if they were the same man, which they were, except when O'Nolan was writing, which is when he became one of the others, depending on what he was writing (novels as

O'Brien, journalism as na gCopaleen, which means "of the little horses"). There were even others, as he apparently used a different name every time he took up the pen, which he did often, sometimes as Count O'Blather, or John James Doe, or Brother Barnabas, or George Knowall.

My wife is unmoved; she will not have Etain in the house.

After a while I realize that the problem is the word *woo*. It is a word that may be applied to your wife and your wife only if you have a wife, she is saying without saying. She is a subtle woman, which is part of the reason I wooed her some years ago, and won her from various rivals, who did not woo so well, and went away, one may say, full of rue.

I spent some time after that saying *woo*, which is a very fine word, rife with meaning, and emitted with a lift from the lips, like *whee* and *who* or *no*. By chance I happened to be saying *woo* in the presence of my new son Joseph, a curious young man three months of age. Like his father he is intrigued by sounds, and soon enough he too was saying *woo*, and then my other new son, Liam, also three months old, picked it up, and the three of us were wooing to beat the band, although then Liam burst into tears, and had to be carried away to another room for milk.

Joe and I kept it up, though; he is an indefatigable fellow. After a while he switched to *who*, and I went with him, to see where this would go, and it went back and forth between us for a while, and then it went to *whee*, and then back to *woo*, and then my wife came back in the room and found us wooing like crazy men. By then it was Joe's turn for a suckle, and off he went, and I went downstairs to raid cattle in Cuailnge, and ponder Oenghus, and feast at Bricriu, and woo Etain, of whom the less said the better.

The wooing of Etain demands a certain familiarity with the Gaelic tongue, which has fascinated me since I was a boy in my grandmother's lap listening to the swell and swing of Irish from her lips, which more often than you might expect had Gaelic oaths on them, as she was a shy woman with a sharp temper, though gentle as the night is long, and much mourned by many to this day. I still hear her voice on windy nights, banshee nights, saying to me gently, *Bí i do bhuachaill maith*, be a good boy, or *Go mbeannaí Dia thú*, God bless you. So partly in memory of my grandmother, a McCluskey before she was a Clancey giving her daughter to a Doyle, I have been marching through the thickets of the Irish tongue, the second oldest in Europe behind Basque, and the cold hard fact is that the Gaelic language is a most confusing creature, and although I don't understand very much of it, I read about it at every opportunity, and have been able to note several interesting observations on small scraps of paper, which are then distributed willy-nilly in various pants pockets, emerging here and there like crumpled fish, and reminding me that I had meant to write an essay on the topic at, or more accurately in, hand.

Thus this essay, which was supposed to be about the fact that there is no way to say the words *yes* and *no* in Gaelic, but which has swerved unaccountably into a disquisition about sounds, of which some are exuberant, like Joe's *woo*, and some affirmative, like *'sea*, which is Gaelic for *it is*, and *yes* and *si* and *ja* and *oui*, which are English and Spanish and German and French for *yes*, which there is no way to say in Gaelic, try as you might.

Is it sayable in the Irish?

Níl—it is not.

Níl is as fascinating as *'sea* to me, especially so lately because my daughter, a rebellious angel, age three, is fixated on *no*, which she says often, in different accents, with various degrees of vehemence. She says it morning, noon, and night, particularly at night, when she wakes up screaming *no no no no no* and answers *nooooo* when I ask what is the matter. Sometimes she says *neuwh*, which is a sort of *no*, and which is said usually after she has been watching *Mary Poppins* and is afflicted with a sort of stiffening of the upper lip, which prevents proper pronunciation of simple words like *no*. It is interesting that she is riveted by *no*, because her brother Liam is riveted by *ho*, which is the only word he owns at the moment. Like a geyser he emits *ho!* regularly and then subsides. I expect him to pick up *no* pretty soon, his sister being a whiz at it and the boys certain to learn at her knee, and then Joe will get *no* too and then my children will be saying *no* to beat the band, not to mention the thin stretched rubber of their father's patience, which they hammer upon like a brittle drum.

But their father is in the basement at the moment musing over the fact that Gaelic is the only language in Europe that always uses *tú* (*thou*) when speaking to one person, and *sibh* (*you*) for more than one, which habit, he thinks, reflects a certain native friendliness in the tongue and in its speakers; and he further puzzles over the fact that Irish counts in twenties, not tens, and muses even further that Gaelic, at least in Ireland, has no terms of bourgeois respect, as English and Spanish and German do, with *mister* and *señor* and *herr,* which makes him wonder about Irish independence as well as rural isolation. Also he spends a good deal of time pondering ogham—the alphabet used in Ireland for writing on wood and stone before A.D. 500 or so, when Christianity and the Latin alphabet rode into Ireland together on strong winds—and the fact that Gaelic has perhaps sixty phonemes, which are sounds that convey meaning, and of which there are perhaps forty-four in English, a comparative fact that makes him wonder about the width, so to speak, of these respective languages, a width that is also reflected in the spelling and pronunciation of terms in each tongue: I might say of Liam, for example, that he is *an buachaill,* the boy, and roll the Gaelic off my tongue like a song but pop the English out like a button, rather like *ho!* which is what Liam is saying as I am calling him *an buachaill.*

Further I am fascinated by the fact that Gaelic is a language in love with nouns, as can be seen with a phrase that often occurs to me when I think about my daughter's and my sons' futures, *tá eagla orm,* which in English would be *I fear* but in Gaelic is *fear is upon me,* which it is, like a demon between my shoulders. To exorcise it

I sometimes whistle; in English, *I whistle,* just so, but in Gaelic, *ligim fead,* I let a whistle, or *táim ag feadaíl,* I am at whistling.

I am at whistling a great deal these days, it turns out, trying to get the fear off me. For I am terrified of the fates that may befall my children—fates over which I have no power at all, not the slightest, other than keeping my little new people close to me in the presence of cars and dogs and such. So there are times now, I can honestly say, for I am sometimes an honest man, and admiring always of honesty, that I am exhausted by, and frightened for, my raft of children, and in the wee hours of the morning, when I am up with one or another of the small people, I sometimes, to be honest, find myself wondering what it might have been like to not have so many.

It would have been lonely.

I know this.

I know it in my heart, in my bones, in the chalky exhausted shiver of my soul. For there were many nights before my children came to me on magic wooden boats from seas unknown that I wished desperately for them, that I cried because they had not yet come; and now that they are here I know I pay for them every minute with fear for their safety and horror at the prospect of losing them to disease and accidents and the harsh fingers of the Lord, who takes whomever he wishes, at which time he alone appoints, and leaves huddled and broken the father and the mother, who begged for the joy of these round faces groping for milk in the dark. So as I trudge upstairs to hold my daughter in my lap, and rub my old chapped hands across the thin sharp blades of her shoulders, and shuffle with sons on shoulders in the blue hours of night, waiting patiently for them to belch like river barges, or hear Joe happily blowing bubbles of spit in his crib simply because he can do it and is pretty proud of himself about the whole thing, or hear Liam suddenly say *ho!* for no reason other than Liamly joy at the sound of his own voice like a bell in his head, I say *yes* to them, *yes yes yes*, and to exhaustion I say *yes*, and to the puzzling wonder of my wife's love I say *O yes*, and to horror and fear and joy I say *yes*, to rich cheerful chaos that leads me sooner to the grave and happier along that muddy grave road I say *yes*, to my absolute surprise and with unbidden tears I say *yes yes O yes*.

Is this a mystery and a joy beyond my wisdom?

'*Sea*—it is.

Call for Entries

Loyola Press is accepting submissions for an annual series collecting the best Catholic writing, edited by Brian Doyle, essayist and editor of *Portland Magazine*. We are looking for writing that is true, remarkable, and Catholic minded, be it in the form of an essay, article, memoir, rant, prayer, sermon, homily, literary exploration, travelogue, etc. This writing can come from magazines, newspapers, Web sites, books, journals, colleges, seminars, schools, seminaries, monasteries, newsrooms, theaters—everywhere.

Please send any articles, stories, essays, columns, or editorials from any publications—Catholic or secular—that particularly struck you, as well as poems, excerpts from books, and unpublished or yet-to-be published writings to:

Brian Doyle
Portland Magazine
University of Portland
5000 N. Willamette Blvd.
Portland OR 97203
bdoyle@up.edu

Please include contact information for the rights holder if you have it. If your piece is selected, you will receive a copy of the book in which it appears.